Leading a
Friends Helping Friends
Peer Program

by

Carol Painter

Copyright 1989
Educational Media Corporation®

Library of Congress Catalog Card No. 89-80324

ISBN 0-932796-29-X

Printing (Last Digit)

9 8 7 6 5 4 3 2

Publisher—

**Educational Media Corporation®
P.O. Box 21311
Minneapolis, MN 55421-0311**

(612) 781-0088

Production editor—

Don L. Sorenson

Graphic design—

Earl Sorenson

Dedication

To all those who have come before
and to those who will come after.

About the Author

Carol Painter, M.A., has been a high school counselor for one decade and has been involved in training peer counselors for most of those years. Since 1986, she has been the peer counselor coordinator for the Flagstaff Unified School District, developing and implementing a peer counselor program. Carol has been very involved in preparing other professionals to lead peer counselor programs and has made numerous presentations at professional conferences. She has a deep and personal commitment to the concept of friends helping friends.

Carol lives with her husband and daughter in Flagstaff, Arizona.

Table of Contents

A Letter to Advisors

Dear Peer Counselor Advisor:

Because it is so true what we give out comes back to us, the advisor of a peer counselor program is blessed many times over by the ripple effect created with a program such as this. There are many priceless gifts that come with this great undertaking. There is the deeply satisfying knowledge we are truly and positively touching other lives. There are the endless opportunities for personal growth. Most of all, there is the love that grows among a group of young people and their advisor as they strive to become fully themselves and to give that gift to others.

The idea of friends helping friends is as old as time. What is a relatively new idea, though, is teaching helping and communication skills to young people so they are able to be more effective friends and helpers. As a high school counselor, I would never again have the courage to be a counselor in a school without the support of a peer counselor program. We *know* kids listen to other kids, for better or for worse. A peer counselor program allows us to harness the power of *positive* peer pressure.

Helping and communication skills can be taught to people of any age as long as they care for the well being of others and are excited by becoming all they can be. When young people recognize they can make a difference for others, it has a profound effect on their lives. Suddenly it becomes only natural to reach out to others and to express concern and support. Just as suddenly, these same young people find themselves digging deeper into themselves. There they discover a greater understanding and acceptance of themselves and others. With that, they develop a desire to know more, to do more, and to be more.

For all you will do and give to others, my heartfelt respect and deep gratitude are yours.

May you always walk in love and light,

Carol Painter

Chapter 1

An Overview of Peer Counseling

I have always chosen the title of peer counselor rather than peer helper, or some other designated term, because I like the seriousness of the role it signifies. A peer counselor *is* a counselor in all the finest meanings of the term. Peer counselors *never* give advice but rather listen with empathy and respect. Peer counselors do not solve problems for others but rather facilitate deeper awareness, leading others to their own solution seeking. Peer counselors provide a caring source of support and information among a community of students. Peer counselors learn to recognize their limits, and they know when and how to make referrals to professionals within the school and community. Peer counselors build a bridge between the community of students and the community of helping adults. A peer counselor is a peer helper is a friend.

A peer counselor can be a person of any age working within any setting, such as a school, a church, a business, or a community. Although the *Friends Helping Friends* program was developed for a high school setting, the materials are applicable in any setting, and the programs can be adapted for a variety of purposes.

In his guide you will find materials and processes for developing an extensive peer counselor program. You will find information and materials to assist in the selection of peer counselors. This guide, together with the student manual, will help you provide over fifty hours of training to peer counselors in three areas: philosophy of helping, communication skills, and background topics. The sections which deal with these areas are Helper Development, Skills Development, and Topic Development.

Lesson plans are provided in this guide for each day of training. In addition, you will find materials for developing programs and placements such as individual referrals, a new student buddy program, a support group program, a "special friend" program with students at the elementary level, and a junior high/high school special placement program with emotionally handicapped students. In addition, you will find two different series of classroom presentations. One is a substance abuse prevention program with fourth graders, and the other one is a transition to the junior high program with sixth graders.

The lesson plans for Helper Development and Skills Development training include activities to introduce and extend discussion on each concept and to provide additional personal experiences. The additional personal experiences come in the form of "Challenges." Challenges are given as "homework" at the end of each of the Helper and Skills Development training sessions. These effectively keep the training ideas uppermost in the peer counselors' minds from one training session to the next. They also provide an excellent opportunity for the peer counselors to "walk their talk." Challenges tend to stimulate lively discussion, and they personalize the training experience. When Challenge experiences are shared through a journal, it provides the peer counselor advisor with a much more individual look at each peer counselor's progress during training.

At the completion of each unit of Skills Development, the peer counselors form training triads, consisting of the roles of "helper," "friend," and "observer." Using role play topics at first and personal experiences later, training triads give the peer counselors an opportunity to practice skills in an actual helping conversation. Roles are rotated within the triads so each peer counselor experiences each position. A skills chart is also a part of each skills unit, and it provides direction to the observer and feedback to the helper.

In training peer counselors, it is important to present concepts as free from the use of terminology as possible. Every effort is made to express ideas in language as "normal" as possible, so the peer counselors do not begin to sound "different." Their language will change to some extent as will their approach to situations as a result of their training. The changes in their language need to be minimized rather than exaggerated, so the program remains one with which other students are comfortable. It is their very specialness as young people that makes peer counselors so effective. Any attempt to turn them into "little professors" will only lessen their effectiveness.

The material in the Topic Development section covers those areas in which peer counselors need to be knowledgeable so that their first response in a situation will be helpful. The topics which are included are those which my experience has shown are likely to surface for the peer counselors in a year of working with many other students. Although this section is intended to be supplemented by guest speakers and experts from the school or from private and community agencies, it does provide a reference for the peer counselors after training is completed.

One of the topics covered in this section is suicide prevention and intervention. Adults will often have concerns about the advisability of asking peer counselors to take a role in a suicide prevention and intervention program. My feelings about this issue became very clear when a student suicide occurred at one of the high schools where I was directing a peer counselor program. In addition to the grief experienced by large numbers of students, the suicide also stimulated other suicide attempts as well as huge numbers of suicidal gestures and threats.

Many students turned to peer counselors during this terribly trying and painful time, and it was a difficult time for all of us. One of the peer counselors, a young woman, was involved over a period of time with several students who were showing strong suicidal ideation. After awhile, her mother understandably became concerned at her involvement with these students and its affect on her. Her response was, "Mom, these people are my friends, and I would be involved with them whether I was a peer counselor or not. The only difference is without my training as a peer counselor I would be a nervous wreck by now!" After a suicide in a school the size of ours, statistically we could expect to see *two* more suicides before the year was out. Although the suicidal behavior remained at a high level for the entire year, there were *no more suicides!* The difference between what was and what could have been was largely attributed by the professionals in the school to the work of the peer counselors and to the safety net provided by the peer counselor program.

Within a school setting, it must be clearly communicated to peer counselors that all situations dealing with suicidal or abused students *must* be referred immediately to the peer counselor advisor or to another counselor or agency. Having a plan for effective referrals by peer counselors is a top priority for the peer counselor advisor, and this plan needs to be developed within each school or organization before beginning a program.

Confidentiality is also of critical importance to a peer counselor program, and the reputation the peer counselors develop regarding confidentiality will quickly make or break a program. However, this is a concept peer counselors understand well. They live in a world where rumors are frequent occurrences and where they see "trusted" friends betraying confidences. When the importance of confidentiality is backed by a policy that requires a peer counselor to be removed from a program if a break in confidentiality occurs, peer counselors handle this responsibility in an extremely admirable way.

The role of the peer counselor advisor is an obviously important one to the success of a program. It is time we stop asking school counselors to run a peer counselor program "on the side," in addition to all their other duties and responsibilities. It is also time the position of peer counselor advisor be recognized as a full-time position within a single school. No other counseling position reaches as many students or has the level of financial accountability as the peer counselor advisor.

A full-time position for the peer counselor advisor helps to insure time is available for work with the peer counselors and with the students who are referred by the peer counselors. In addition, it allows the peer counselor advisor to expand the training of peer counselors to include more students and to expand the program to include more peer counselors. Over the years, peer counselors have repeatedly said to me *all* students should receive the training they have received.

Ideally, a peer counselor training course would be made available to all students who were interested. Then the peer counselors for the following year would be selected from among the students in the training courses. While being a peer counselor could be a good experience for most students, it is critically important to remember a peer counselor must also be good for a program! A peer counselor program will grow and develop when the adults who are involved in working with peer counselors are impressed with their dependability and skill. With this approach to training, students who are interested at least can receive the training, even if they are not chosen for a program.

One of the most important functions of the peer counselor advisor is to see the peer counselors are never burdened or stressed beyond their capacity. Although they are extraordinarily special young people, they are *still young people* who are also dealing with all the trials of being adolescents. However, in my experience, when peer counselors know the peer counselor advisor is there to support them and when they know they are to refer a situation anytime they feel overwhelmed, this sets the stage for healthy ways of dealing with situations. It is my experience the more training peer counselors have, the more likely they are to recognize their limits and to make referrals. As adults, we also need to remember it is the responsibility the peer counselors want and like! It satisfies their need to feel worthwhile at a time when there are not many opportunities for that.

So much can be accomplished with a peer counselor program! This is true whether it is a small program with only one task or a large program with many complex aims. The most crucial step is deciding whether to actually begin a peer counselor program! Once this step is taken and a peer counselor program is established, it will grow and develop to meet the needs of the school and community of which it will become an integral part.

Chapter 2

A Model for a High School Peer Counselor Program

Structure: Two Possible Approaches

Approach (1): The peer counselor training course

The peer counselor training course is available to all students who are interested. However, a self-eliminating screening process is established in order to insure a high level of interest and dedication among the students in the training course. For example, those interested in taking the training course could be required to attend a couple of evening sessions or to write an essay on the value of peer counseling.

The training course is a semester course awarding elective academic credit and meeting daily at a specific time and place. The training course is preferably offered during the spring semester, and it is the primary method of selection for new peer counselors.

The selection of peer counselors for the following year is based upon their performance within the training course. It is advisable to also use the teacher evaluation and peer evaluation processes, described in the chapter titled "Selection of Peer Counselors," in order to obtain feedback on how others perceive the students who apply as peer counselors. One of the difficulties of this method of selection is the new peer counselors are selected before the training course ends. This is difficult for the students in the training course who are not selected as peer counselors. However, this can be handled effectively by talking with the students about this situation at the beginning of the course and also again as selection time approaches.

The students selected as peer counselors from the training course are enrolled in the peer counselor practicum course for the following year. Peer counselors may take the practicum course for credit for more than one year. As advanced peer counselors, these students function as peer instructors in coordination with the peer counselor advisor. After a review of training within the practicum course at the beginning of the year, the peer counselors begin their programs and services to students.

(Note: If this approach is used, it is advisable to give the training course a name which does not use the term peer counselor. Otherwise, there will be great confusion on the part of teachers and students as to who is a peer counselor and who is in training as a peer counselor!)

Approach (2): The peer counselor training/practicum course

The students who have been selected as peer counselors the previous spring are enrolled at the beginning of the year in the peer counselor training/practicum course. However, only those students who successfully complete the training will be assigned placements as peer counselors. The peer counselor training/practicum course awards elective academic credit. It is a class which meets daily at a specific time and place throughout the entire school year. A peer counselor may take the training/practicum course for credit for more than one year. In this event, these advanced peer counselors function as peer instructors in coordination with the peer counselor advisor. The advanced peer counselors also are available for individual work or group facilitation from the beginning of the year. In this way it is not necessary to wait until the new group of peer counselors is trained to begin providing services to students.

Training

Approach (1): The peer counselor training course

The training of peer counselors is completed during the semester-long peer counselor training course. After training in Helper Development, Skills Development, and Topic Development has been completed, the peer counselor training course functions as a support group in which students develop their skills in group leadership.

Approach (2): The peer counselor training/practicum course

While the majority of the training for peer counselors occurs during the first 10-12 weeks of the school year, continued training, particularly in group leadership, occurs throughout the year.

Placements and Programs

Both Approaches

All programs and placements, with the exception of the new student buddy program, are implemented after the peer counselors complete their training. The new student buddy program can be successfully implemented at any time of the year.

1. **New student buddy program:** When new students enroll in the school, the counseling secretary sends for peer counselors to welcome them. The peer counselors take new students to their lockers, to their teachers for signatures, to get their IDs and library cards, and so forth. The peer counselors also meet new students for lunch the first day in order to introduce them to other students.

2. **Individual referrals at the high school:** Students may self-refer or be referred by a parent, teacher, counselor, administrator, or friend for individual work with a peer counselor. The duration of the placement is best monitored by the peer counselor in consultation with the peer counselor advisor. If referrals are made

by someone other than the students themselves, they are *invited* to work with a peer counselor, but they are always given the option on whether or not to accept.

3. **Support group programs, or student assistance programs:** Teams made up of two or three peer counselors facilitate a support group under the direct supervision of a school counselor or other professional counselor. Once the groups begin, each group meets weekly for the duration of the school year. Groups are offered both at the high school and the junior high level.

4. **Elementary "special friend" program:** Each peer counselor is matched with an elementary student who has been referred by a teacher, counselor, or parent. As with all peer counselor placements, the elementary students are given the option as to whether or not they want to participate. The peer counselor and the "special friend" meet once a week at the elementary school for discussion and activities designed by the peer counselor to meet the needs of the "special friend."

5. **Junior high/high school special placement program:** Each peer counselor is matched with a student in the emotionally handicapped program in the junior high or high school. Although the students are referred by a teacher, counselor, or parent, they are given the option on whether or not to participate. The peer counselor and the student meet once a week at the junior high or high school for discussion and activities designed by the peer counselor to meet the needs of the student.

6. **Substance abuse prevention classroom presentations:** Teams of two or three peer counselors give a four-session series of presentations in fourth grade classrooms on self-esteem, feelings, communication, and substance abuse.

7. **Transition to the junior high classroom presentations:** In the spring, teams of three or four peer counselors give presentations in sixth grade classrooms to prepare the students for the changes they will experience in the

junior high setting. The presentations also include a rumor control activity and a refusal skills demonstration.

8. **Other alternatives:** Alternative placements for the peer counselors include group or individual work within the alternative high school or program for pregnant students. Group or individual work is also provided for at-risk students in a drop-out prevention program.

9. **Community activities:** The peer counselors may also work on teen-age crisis phone lines, as big brothers or big sisters within the community agency, or by writing articles for the school or community newspaper.

A Typical Week's Schedule

Once training is completed within the practicum course or training/practicum course, the following schedule is used:

Monday:
A "support group session" is held in which the peer counselor advisor is the group leader and the peer counselors are the group members. These group sessions serve as continued training, and they allow the peer counselors to further develop their group leadership skills by observing the responses of the peer counselor advisor. The "support group sessions" also serve effectively to provide an outlet for the peer counselors in dealing with events in their own lives. Processing of these group sessions includes a discussion of the group dynamics which occurred or are likely to occur.

Tuesday:
Support groups, or student assistance groups, are held. Some of the peer counselors may travel to other schools for their groups. If groups are held on a rotating schedule, some of the peer counselors' groups will meet during a class period other than the peer counselor course. In this case, the peer counselors may use this class time to do work for the regular class they will miss while in group. Or, if

they have an individual referral, they may work with that student during this time if prior arrangements have been made with the student's teacher.

Wednesday:
The peer counselors work individually with their junior high or high school special placement students. Some of the peer counselors will travel to other schools to fulfill this placement.

Thursday:
The peer counselors work individually with their elementary "special friends." They will travel to the designated elementary school in order to fulfill this placement.

Friday:
Assessment of the week's activities and planning for the following week occurs. The peer counselors are given preparation time so group teams can meet and preparation for other placements can occur. At times, continuing training is offered through guest speakers or classroom activities. Early in the year, this day is also used as an additional "support group session." Later in the year, the peer counselors will travel to elementary schools to give classroom presentations on this day. (Note: If there are conflicts on Fridays with other school activities, Mondays also work well for classroom presentations.)

Chapter 3

Basics and a Beginning

Goal and Objectives of a
Peer Counseling Program

Goal:

To establish a specially selected and trained segment of the student population which serves as a liaison between the adult and student community and which supplements and complements the services available from the professional counseling staff.

Objectives:

- To provide positive peer role modeling to students of all ages.

- To enhance self-esteem among students of all ages through interaction with peer counselors.

- To alleviate stress among students by providing helpers who are more readily available or are seen as more accessible.

- To provide a bridge between the student population and the population of helping adults.

- To increase communication of needs and feelings between students and adults.

- To provide positive peer pressure in prevention oriented activities.

- To provide the healing environment of support groups in which friends help friends.

Getting Started

In laying the ground work for a peer counselor program at your school, you will begin by meeting with the members of the counseling department to present your proposal and to solicit their feedback. It is important to emphasize the program is designed to enhance rather than replace their efforts. Focus on the ways a peer counselor program would assist the counseling department as a group and as individuals. Actively problem-solve for solutions to any obstacles identified.

Remember people support what they help to create. Ask the counseling department to develop a profile of a peer counselor program which would meet the needs of your school and community. Develop a proposal which is supported by the entire counseling department. As a group, present this proposal to your district administration/school board.

Your proposal will be most effective if it includes a statement of need from the students. A survey of your student body may help you to obtain this information. You will need to be prepared to discuss with your district administration/school board how you will select and train peer counselors and also how the peer counselors will interact with other students.

The precedent for a peer counselor program can be effectively established by identifying other school districts in your state or region which have programs. Your state department of education, or the National Peer Helpers Association, 2370 Market Street, Room 120, San Francisco, CA 94114, can help with this.

The precedent for giving credit to the peer counselor courses can be established by comparing them to other programs such as nurse's training, where the students are taught in the classroom and then apply their knowledge "on the job" in the hospital setting. The peer counselor courses are applied psychology courses with a laboratory emphasis! Since communication in interpersonal relationships is the most basic of all education skills, the peer counselor courses teach the most fundamental of skills.

Chapter 4

Selection of Peer Counselors

Publicity and Recruitment

Unless you are fortunate enough to be using peer counselor training courses as your method of selection, begin your recruitment process with a publicity campaign to include all of the following elements:

1. Run 8 1/2 x 11" posters on your school's copy machine with a message like the following one:

"MAKE A DIFFERENCE!"
BE A PEER COUNSELOR NEXT YEAR

**PICK UP YOUR APPLICATION
IN THE COUNSELING OFFICE
DEADLINE: MARCH 21**

- **Important note:** In addition to distributing these around the school, place a copy in each teacher's mail box and ask them to post one in each classroom!

2. Run announcements such as the following ones for several days in the daily bulletin:

  - A peer counselor receives special training in communication skills and personal relationships. If you are interested in being a part of this program for next year, pick up an application in the counseling office.

  - A peer counselor has the opportunity to work with other students in our support group program at the high school and junior high school. Applications are available in the counseling office.

  - A peer counselor works with elementary students in our "special friend" program and is also eligible to be part of big brothers and big sisters. Applications are available in the counseling office.

  - A peer counselor gives presentations to fourth graders as part of our substance abuse prevention program. A peer counselor also gives presentations to sixth graders in our transition to the junior high program. Applications are available in the counseling office.

  - A peer counselor has an opportunity to *make a difference* in our school and community. Applications are available in the counseling office.

  - *Tomorrow* is the deadline for returning peer counselor applications to the counseling office.

  - *Today* is the deadline for peer counselor applications.

3. Do a poll of the student body, asking them to identify the students they would want to talk with if they had a problem. Notify and *congratulate* the students whose names appear most frequently. Invite them to apply for the program.

4. Once you have a program established, ask the present peer counselors to each recruit one male and one female to apply for the program.

Applications

Put together application packets using the following material, after having it typed or printed on your school's letterhead:

Description of the Peer Counselor Program

We know when students have a concern or problem, they will usually turn first to one of their peers and next perhaps to an adult. A peer is able to share and identify with their needs and problems in a special way. When the peers have been specially trained in helping skills, their ability to make a positive difference becomes very significant. This is the philosophy behind the peer counselor program.

Students are selected as peer counselors based on their ability to relate well with all people—adults as well as other students. Equally important are such characteristics as responsibility, maturity, common sense, and consistency in follow-through. The students' cumulative credits and cumulative grade point average are also taken into consideration since peer counselors miss some class time as part of their work in this program.

To apply for the program, students must complete and return the application form which requires a parent/guardian signature. In addition, the applicants are required to distribute evaluation forms to each of their teachers. Those chosen as finalists will be given a panel interview with the peer counselor advisor, school counselors, and two peer counselors.

When students are selected as peer counselors, they are enrolled in the peer counselor training/practicum course which is a course awarding elective academic credit. During this course, the peer counselors will be trained in philosophy of helping, listening and communication skills, assertiveness, confrontation, and problem-solving skills. Training will also include topics such as group leadership, chemical dependency, children of alcoholics, suicide prevention and intervention, grief, rape, families, divorce, stepfamilies, eating disorders, family violence, teenage pregnancy, and AIDS.

After the peer counselors' training is completed, they will work individually with students at the high school, junior high, and elementary levels. They will also facilitate a support group at the high school or junior high school level under the direct supervision of a school counselor or other professional counselor. In addition, they will give two series of classroom presentations at the elementary school level. One is a substance abuse prevention program for fourth graders, and the other is a transition to the junior high program for sixth graders. In addition, the peer counselors are also eligible to become a big brother or big sister within our community agency.

A peer counselor has the opportunity to be a positive, supportive influence in the lives of many other people. As importantly, peer counselors usually find what they learn about themselves during training and as they work with other people enhances their ability to relate with others in new and exciting ways.

Carol Painter
Peer Counselor Advisor

Letter to Applicants

Dear Peer Counselor Applicant:

I am really pleased you are interested in becoming a peer counselor!

Here are the guidelines you will need to follow in completing your application:

1. Carefully respond to the questions on the Peer Counselor Application Form and return it to the counseling office before the deadline shown at the bottom of the page. Notice a parent or guardian signature is required on the application form.

2. Your response to the question of ethnic background on the application form is optional. However, this information is used in attempting to achieve a good ethnic mix in the program.

3. Distribute all six copies of the Peer Counselor Teacher Evaluation Form to your present teachers. Before giving them to your teachers, fill in your name and ID number. Be sure to give the evaluation forms to your teachers immediately so they have time to complete them before the deadline.

If you have a class which started second semester and if the teacher does not know you well enough to answer the questions on the evaluation form, you may give it to a first semester teacher instead. However, only do this with the permission of your second semester teacher and indicate the change on your application form.

As application forms and teacher evaluation forms are returned, they will be thoroughly studied, and both student and adult input on each applicant will be taken. This is a lengthy process. After it is completed, the students who are seen as the strongest candidates—the finalists—will be contacted to set up a time for a panel interview.

Choosing the finalists is the most difficult part of this process. The students who are interested in being peer counselors are always a very special and select group of people.

This, together with the fact such large numbers of people apply for the program, makes the competition for the openings very strong.

What we are looking for are people with the qualities listed on the evaluation form who can also work well with people individually, in groups, and in classroom presentations. However, these qualities are present in people with a lot of different personality styles. So there is never one "kind" of person we are seeking. Instead, we are looking for those people who in their own way demonstrate all the qualities important for a peer counselor to possess.

If it should happen you are not selected for the program, it is extremely important you do not take this as a rejection of who you are, as if it indicates there is something wrong with you. If you are not selected for the program, it does not mean you do not have the qualities we are looking for, but rather another person was seen as having them to a greater degree with a broader group of people.

Because of the large number of applicants, it is not possible to meet with each person individually before choosing finalists. I want to assure you every other possible way of gathering information and a great deal of time is spent before a decision is made on who the finalists will be. Again because of numbers, those who have not been chosen as finalists will be notified in a form letter.

The size of the program has grown in the last few years and includes as many peer counselors as possible at the present time. There have always been more people interested in becoming peer counselors than there have been available openings. I urge you to maintain your interest in being a peer counselor and to follow through with your application. It is the specialness of the many different peer counselors that has always been the strength of our program.

Thank you for your interest. You are what makes our school the special place it is!

Sincerely,

Carol Painter
Peer Counselor Advisor

Peer Counselor Application Form

CUM CR _____
CGPA _____
(Office Use Only)

Name _____

Address _____

ID No. _____ Phone Number _____

Ethnic Background _____

Write a short description of an experience you have had that would help you in being an effective peer counselor.

Describe the qualities of an effective peer counselor.

List the groups to which you belong, both in school and out of school.

Which group do you find to be the most rewarding? Why?

Describe three values that are guiding principles in your life.

Please list the teachers in whose classes you are enrolled this semester.

_____   _____

_____   _____

_____   _____

_____

Parent/Guardian Signature   Date

Please return this form to the counseling office by March 21.

Peer Counselor Teacher Evaluation Form

Name _____ ID No. _____

This student is making application as a peer counselor for next year. Please evaluate this person in each of the categories listed below. *This information will remain confidential* and will be used to assist in the selection of the best applicants for the program.

Rating Scale: 4—Excellent 3—Good 2—Fair 1—Poor

4 3 2 1   1. How dependable is this person in meeting responsibilities and following through with tasks?

4 3 2 1   2. How effectively does this person deal with personal problems?

4 3 2 1   3. How well does this person seem to listen to and understand others?

4 3 2 1   4. How well does this person demonstrate effective decision-making skills?

4 3 2 1   5. How honest is this person?

4 3 2 1   6. To what extent does this person show strong, healthy self-esteem and self-confidence?

4 3 2 1   7. How much leadership potential does this person demonstrate?

4 3 2 1   8. How warm and accepting is this person with those of different interests and attitudes?

4 3 2 1   9. How open and out-going is this person?

Yes   No   10. Does this person have an attendance or tardy problem?

Please describe how you feel this person would function as a peer counselor:

_____

Teacher Signature

Please return to the counseling office by March 21.

Memo to the Faculty

At the same time students are picking up application packets, send the following memo to the faculty:

Date: March 3
To: Faculty
From: Carol Painter
RE: Peer Counselor Selection

The students who are applying as peer counselors for next year will again be bringing evaluation forms to you to be completed. I thank you in advance for your feedback! It makes all the difference in choosing the strongest applicants for the program.

A peer counselor needs to be strong in the personal qualities listed on the evaluation form. A peer counselor needs to be able to work well with elementary, junior high, and high school students, as well as with adults. Peer counselors must be able to work with others individually, in groups, and through classroom presentations. This is a lot to ask of any individual, but each year it seems more and more students with these qualities apply. The responses you make on the evaluation form help in making distinctions among the applicants.

If you are given evaluation forms by students whom you have only known a short time and you can not accurately answer the questions, you may refer them to their first semester teachers to complete the evaluation form. Please be sure to let the students know since they have instructions on how to handle this.

If a student gives you an evaluation form at the last minute and you cannot meet the deadline, I will understand. In that case, please return it to me as soon as you possibly can.

Thanks for all your help!

Reminder to Applicants

When you begin receiving teacher evaluation forms for a student, this will alert you a person has decided to apply for the program. However, it is my experience some students will forget to turn in their application form. About three days before the deadline, send a note like the following one to these students:

Dear Peer Counselor Applicant,

Although I am receiving teacher evaluation forms for you, I have not yet received your application form. The application form was in the same packet as the teacher evaluation forms, and it requires a parent or guardian signature. The **deadline** for turning in the application form is **Wednesday, March 21.** Please let me know if you have changed your mind about applying for the program or if there is a problem in having a parent or guardian signature by that time.

Thanks!

Carol Painter
Peer Counselor Advisor

Peer Counselor Evaluation

There have been many situations in which I have found students who are seen in a *very* favorable light by adults are not seen in the same positive way by their peers. It is important to have a balance in the feedback you are receiving for each applicant.

Once you have a program established, ask the present peer counselors to evaluate each applicant. Because they will be extremely sensitive to doing this in the most responsible and caring way, introduce the evaluation process with a statement like the following one:

"As you all know, I am receiving feedback on all of the applicants for next year from each of their teachers. It is important to me to have feedback on all of the applicants from some of their peers as well. I have a form with each of the applicants names on it, and I would like you to tell me the strengths and weaknesses *as you see them* for each applicant. There is also a place where you can make general comments."

"I know this can be a difficult request to make of you. I feel it is extremely important. As adults, we know students in a different way than you know each other. In order to insure peer counselors are people other students trust and feel accepted by, I would like you to tell me how you see each of the applicants as a result of your experiences with them. As you do this, know your comment is only *part* of the feedback I am receiving. No comment by any one person will keep an applicant out of the program. After all of the feedback is compiled, a clear picture usually develops for each applicant, and one person's comments are only a part of that picture. I know each of you will do all you can to give me as balanced a picture of each person as possible. Be honest in your assessments, even if they are negative."

Peer Counselor Evaluation Form

Peer Counselor Signature
_____

Applicant's Name	Strength	Weakness	General Comments
_____	_____	_____	_____
_____	_____	_____	_____
_____	_____	_____	_____
_____	_____	_____	_____
_____	_____	_____	_____
_____	_____	_____	_____
_____	_____	_____	_____
_____	_____	_____	_____

Selection of Finalists and Interview Notification

1. After compiling feedback from teachers and peer counselors for each applicant, set up a meeting with the counseling department to make the selection of finalists. Once the finalists have been selected and notified, have them choose a time for an interview from a list of possible times. It is best to hold all the interviews in one day for comparison purposes.

2. If you are doing the interviews during a school day, use a form like the following one as a notification to teachers. The finalists are to bring this form, signed by their teacher, to the interview:

_____ has an appointment to be interviewed as a finalist in the peer counselor selection process at _____ on Monday, March 26 in the Conference Room. If it is possible for this student to be absent from your class at that time, please sign below and allow the student to leave class that day in time for the interview.

Thank you!
Carol Painter

_____
Teacher Signature

Notification of Non-Finalists

The following letter, on school letterhead, is used to notify the students who were not chosen as finalists:

Dear Peer Counselor Applicant,

Thank you for your application and your interest in the peer counselor program. Due to the number of students who applied, it was not possible to include everyone who was interested. I am sorry to tell you that you were not selected for the program for next year.

I encourage you to continue your interest in working with other people, and I believe your concern for others makes you a valuable and contributing part of our school.

If you would like to discuss this decision with me, please contact me through the counseling office.

Sincerely,

Carol Painter
Peer Counselor Advisor

Interview Arrangements

1. Invite all members of the counseling department to be a part of the panel to interview finalists. In addition, select one male and one female peer counselor to be on the panel. Use the following form to obtain permission for the two peer counselors to be absent from classes the day of the interview:

   Lisa has been chosen to be on the panel to interview the finalists for next year's peer counselors. The interviews will be conducted from 8:00 a.m. until about 5:00 p.m. on Monday, March 26, in the Conference Room. If it is possible for her to be absent from your class on that day, please initial below.

   Thank you!
   Carol Painter

   _____ Mrs. Brown

   _____ Mr. Wilson

   _____ Mr. Thompson

   _____ Ms. Smith

   _____ Mr. Franklin

2. A few days before the interviews, send the following reminder to the panel interviewers:

   Just a reminder interviews for peer counselor finalists are this Monday, March 26, from 8:00 a.m. until about 5:00 p.m. in the Conference Room.

   Our first interview begins at 8:15 a.m. Please meet me at 8:00 a.m. in the Conference Room so we can go over the interview questions. We will give 25 interviews, so if we get started late, we'll have a hard time staying on schedule. Our lunch break will be short, from 12:00 to 12:30, so you might want to bring a lunch.

   Thanks so much for your help!
   Carol Painter

Interviews

1. The interview form which follows is used by each interviewer to make note of the actual responses and significant attitudes shown by each finalist in response to the questions. When the interviewers use the rating scale to evaluate the finalist's response on each question and then total those ratings, it gives the panel a place to start in discussion. Before beginning interviews, decide who will ask each question. However, you may want to change questions periodically in order to avoid getting "stale."

Explain the purpose of each question to the interviewers:

- Question 1 assesses how comfortable or natural the finalists are in speaking before groups and also how much experience they have had in doing this.

- Question 2 assesses how warm and outgoing the finalists are and whether they are already doing many of the things expected of peer counselors.

- Question 3 assesses whether the finalists will enjoy working with young people of all age levels. It actually isn't important which level would be the finalist's favorite. It is only important they are open to the value of working with all age groups.

- Question 4 assesses the background of the finalists. How prepared are they, through their own experiences, to understand and accept the needs of others? Also, how actively do the finalists move across the boundaries of "groups" within the school.

- Question 5 assesses the finalists' own substance use and their ability to provide positive role modeling through a "straight" life style. This question is most effective when asked by a peer counselor.

- Question 6 assesses whether the finalists are "natural helpers." The ideal response is one which first acknowledges how the speaker is feeling, next communicates understanding and acceptance, and then perhaps provides a helpful perspective in dealing with the situation. Since the training is designed to teach the peer counselors facilitative ways of responding, this question is not intended to eliminate finalists but to identify the "naturals."

2. Before each interview begins, the peer counselor advisor welcomes and "warms up" the finalist with a statement like the following:

"We feel you are a special person because of your interest in becoming a peer counselor and also because you were chosen as a finalist out of all those who applied. Try to relax and be yourself as much as possible, since that is what brought you here today! We will be asking you several questions. There are no right or wrong answers to these questions, and they are not used in any way to "trap" you. They are just a way for us to get to know you better in the short time we have. You can help us by actively participating with your answers. We will be taking notes as you talk but try not to let that distract you. We are not making any decisions as you talk! We are only writing down the things you say, so we can better remember your interview later."

After each interview, ask the finalists if they have any questions or would like to add anything. Make sure the finalists know how long you will be in interviews and when they will be notified of the final selection.

Peer Counselor Interview Form

Name _____

Phone Number _____ ID No. _____

Rating Scale: 4—Excellent 3—Good 2—Fair 1—Poor

4 3 2 1   1. The peer counselors are asked to speak before groups of people. What experiences have you had in doing this?

4 3 2 1   2. The peer counselors are often asked to talk to someone they have never met before. Can you give examples of times when you have done this?

4 3 2 1   3. The peer counselors work with elementary, junior high, and high school age students. What age group would be your favorite?

4 3 2 1   4. The peer counselors need to be able to relate to many different people with different kinds of problems. What personal experiences are you willing to share that would help you to do this? To what "groups," or cliques, in this school would you have trouble relating?

4 3 2 1   5. The peer counselors give substance abuse prevention classroom presentations to fourth graders. They work to keep kids drug and alcohol free. Do you use alcohol or other drugs?

4 3 2 1   6. Situation: A friend comes to you and is really upset with his/her parents. Your friend says: "My parents are such jerks! I came in a whole 20 minutes late last night, and now I'm grounded for two months!" How would you respond?

After the Interviews

1. At the same time you notify the new peer counselors of their selection, send special notes with a personal message to all the finalists who were not selected.

2. After all the notifications have been made, run announcements congratulating the new peer counselors for the following year. Ask a photographer from the school or community newspaper to do a picture and article. Have individual pictures taken of the new peer counselors so you can have a poster with their pictures and names displayed in the counseling office at the start of the new school year.

3. Send thank you notes to all your panel interviewers.

4. Send the following memo to teachers:

Date:
To: Faculty/Staff
From: Carol Painter
RE: Peer Counselor Selection

Thanks for all your help with peer counselor selection! We had 57 applicants. I know you filled out a lot of evaluation forms! From the 57 applicants, 25 were selected as finalists based on their GPA and cumulative credits, application form, teacher evaluations, counselor evaluations, and peer counselor evaluations. The 25 finalists were given a panel interview, and 15 new peer counselors were selected to bring the total to 20 peer counselors again, since there are 5 juniors returning.

If you have any questions or comments about selection, including disappointment a certain student wasn't chosen or surprise another one was, I would welcome a chance to talk with you.

Thanks once again for your help!

Letter to New Peer Counselors

A few weeks before the peer counselor training/practicum course will begin, mail the following letter to each new peer counselor:

Dear Peer Counselor,

There is so much I am looking forward to in our coming year together. I look forward to getting to know each of you as a person and a friend and to having you know me in the same way. I look forward to the personal growth we will all experience as individuals and as a group. I look forward to our learning to share with one another and to support each other in the good times and in the difficult ones. I especially look forward to knowing we will be touching the lives of others in many significant ways. For me this represents the most valuable use of life because, although it is sometimes a difficult way to live, it is always deeply gratifying and growth producing.

This work is not for everyone simply because not everyone is ready for such an experience. A great deal of effort and thought went into your selection, and I believe you have all the potential to be a truly great peer counselor! For that greatness to be realized, though, you will need increased openness to yourself, to others, and to new ideas. You will need to be prepared to challenge yourself, sometimes daily. You will need to stretch yourself as never before, sometimes putting the needs of others before your own and sometimes putting your own needs before those of others.

We will spend the first ten to twelve weeks of our class in training. When you have successfully completed training, you will be given the opportunity to work with others individually and in groups. You will work at the elementary, junior high, and high school levels. Later in the year, you will also do two different series of classroom presentations at the elementary level.

Our class is not a difficult class in the traditional sense of having to deal with frequent tests, reports, and so on. However, it may be the most challenging class you ever take in the non-traditional sense of having to confront your own prejudices, personal fears, and ability to accept and care for all people.

It is for this reason I am writing to you. If you are not sure you have the level of commitment to this program I appear to expect, I would like you to call me at 555-3333 so we can talk. However, if you are ready to make a commitment to being the best peer counselor you can become, I am delighted!

If you are ready to proceed, please complete and bring the enclosed contract with you the first day of class. On the third day of class, I will ask you to participate in an activity, called "What's My Bag," as a way of introducing yourself to our group. I would like you to decorate a bag on the outside with pictures, words, phrases, or other things that represent the "you" people see on the *outside*. On the inside of this bag, I want you to include the words, pictures, objects, and so on that represent who you are *inside*. We'll have a lot of fun with this so give some thought to "your bag."

Enjoy the rest of your summer! I look forward to welcoming you into the family of peer counselors!

Love,

Carol Painter
Peer Counselor Advisor

Peer Counselor Contract

I am prepared to fully accept the responsibility of being a peer counselor. I understand this responsibility is first to myself. I agree to work to confront my prejudices and personal fears and to develop my abilities to their highest level. I agree to strive for openness and personal honesty in all my actions.

I also understand I have an equal responsibility to others. I agree to work to develop the highest skill level I can achieve. I understand and value the importance of concern and acceptance for all people. I understand the need to recognize my limits, and I accept there will be times when I will need to refer situations to others who have more training and experience.

My personal statement on how I feel about being a peer counselor is as follows:

My goals for myself as a person and as a peer counselor for the coming year are:

1.

2.

3.

_____

Peer Counselor Signature   Date

Chapter 5

Training

As training begins, develop a slide presentation of your training activities and your programs. This slide presentation can then be used as a way of sharing your program with people in your own school and community and from other areas as well.

The following lesson plans are developed for the peer counselor training/practicum course model. With only a few modifications, however, they can be easily adapted for the peer counselor training course as well.

Helper Development (Day 1-7)

Day 1.

Welcome the peer counselors! Begin introductions by doing a go-around in which everyone introduces oneself:

1. by saying their full names (first, middle, and last);

2. by saying their names the way they would like to be called, such as nicknames, as well as explaining any unusual spelling of their names; and

3. either by saying their names the way their parents say them when they are in trouble or the way boyfriends or girlfriends say their names.

The peer counselor advisor goes first.

Make a statement of your expectations for the peer counselors and describe the activities in which the peer counselors will be involved this year. Talk to them about the positive ways in which you expect they will see changes in their lives. Tell them they have joined the family of peer counselors whose slogan is "Once a peer counselor, always a peer counselor." Encourage them to take the risk of trying new behaviors with people because trust is built on taking risks and finding acceptance in its place.

Explain you are going to do a visualization activity with them, so ask the peer counselors to get as comfortable as possible. Then *slowly* give the following directions:

Visualization Activity:
"Close your eyes. Begin to breathe deeply.... Breathe in through your nose and hold the breath for as long as you comfortably can.... Breathe out slowly through slightly parted lips.... As you inhale, picture yourself breathing in peace, love, and joy.... As you exhale, picture yourself breathing out conflict, pain, and worry....(Allow a few moments for this).... Feel a wave of serenity move very slowly down through your body.... And then very slowly back up again.... (Allow a few moments for this.)

Now I want you to picture all of us sitting in a circle in a large open area or room, such as the football field or the gym..... As you sit there, you begin to notice other students coming into the room or area where we are.... They begin lining up quietly behind you..... The thing that catches your attention is these are all really special people.... When you look at them, you realize they are all people who care about others and have a lot to give.... By the time they are all lined up behind you, you see there are 57 students (the number of students who applied as peer counselors) standing quietly behind you.... Then you realize this is how many students applied to be peer counselors, and you realize these are the people who wanted to be sitting where you are now.... As you look around again, you realize what a compliment it is to you that you were chosen as a peer counselor.... You experience again your dedication to being the best peer counselor you can be.... Picture yourself doing the things you want to do and being the peer counselor you want to be as I remain quiet for awhile.... (Allow a few moments for this).... Whenever you are ready, open your eyes and come back to where we are now, feeling strong, relaxed, and good about yourself and the world."

Process:
How did you feel during this visualization?

Explain to the peer counselors the purpose of this activity is not to make them feel guilty about the others who were not chosen. It is to help them focus on the trust placed in them and to encourage their commitment to their new position.

Next, go-around the circle and ask the peer counselors to share their three goals for the year from their peer counselor contract. Collect the contracts after everyone has shared and return them the next day with a personal note. Have the peer counselors keep their contract in the front of a folder provided for them in your classroom.

Hand out copies of the "Challenge Report," located in the Appendix, or explain the method you will use to have the peer counselors respond to Challenges. Explain Challenges are assignments that require the peer counselors to put into practice in their own lives the ideas or skills discussed during training. By having the peer counselors write their responses to each Challenge in journal form, it gives you an individual look at how they are feeling and what they are experiencing during training. Their response to each Challenge should include a description of what they did, how they felt, what reaction they experienced from others, and what they realized as a result of doing the Challenge. Explain you will be collecting their Challenge Reports after every fifth Challenge (or in whatever way you have decided). Give the following Challenge to the peer counselors:

Challenge:
Because we are in the business of making a difference for others, talk to five people today who are alone or who are not being included in the activity going on around them.

Have the peer counselors write this Challenge in the first section of the Challenge Report form, leaving room for their response.

Remind the peer counselors you will be doing the "What's My Bag" activity on the third day.

Day 2.

Ask for discussion or questions on their Challenge of the previous day. What were their experiences? How did they feel? What did they discover?

Tell the peer counselors you are going to do an activity that will allow them to get to know each other better. Tell them you want them to think of a secret about themselves, something they have never told anyone. It can be something they have done or something they have thought. Tell them you will give them a couple minutes to decide what they want to talk about.

After the two minutes are up, announce you are *not* going to ask them to talk about a personal secret! Explain this activity was used to remind them how vulnerable people are when they reveal something personal. This experience will help them look at what they need from the group before they will feel comfortable in sharing personal information.

On a chalkboard or large pad of paper, write the word "FEELINGS." Ask the peer counselors to identify the feelings they experienced when you asked them to talk about a personal secret. Make a list of their responses. Point out their responses are natural ones and are the same responses all people have when revealing themselves to others.

Again on a chalkboard or large pad of paper, write the word "NEEDS." Ask the peer counselors to identify what they need from this group before they will feel safe in talking about anything as personal as a secret. Make a list of their responses. After everyone has had an opportunity to respond, cross out the word "NEEDS," and write the word "NORMS" in its place.

Explain norms are those conditions we agree as a group will be expected behavior when we are together. Ask if everyone can accept as a norm everything on the list. If there is disagreement, change words or phrases until there is consensus. Ask if there are any other norms anyone would like to add to the list. Tell the peer counselors you will make a poster with the norms listed on it as a reminder for the group.

Because trust is one of the needs sure to be listed, use this to introduce and develop the concept of confidentiality. Explain, as peer counselors, they must keep in confidence anything of a personal nature *any* person tells them directly or talks about in a group setting. Being a person others can trust with personal information is an absolutely necessary condition for helping! A peer counselor program that does not have the reputation for maintaining confidentiality is actually no program at all. Explain because a break in confidentiality brings unnecessary pain where a person expected to find help, a peer counselor will immediately and permanently be removed from the program.

Explain you are going to do an activity tomorrow in which everyone will be revealing information about themselves. Confidentiality means keeping private all personal information which is told to you individually or in a group *by anyone.* This means what you hear during this activity will be confidential information, and you are not to share that information with anyone else. However, confidentiality does not mean you cannot talk about *anything* we do! For example, tomorrow you may tell your family, friends, or anyone else we did an activity where we talked about "how we are on the outside and who we are on the inside." This is *not* a break in confidentiality because it gives away no personal information.

Explain there are two exceptions to the rule of confidentiality. One is the peer counselors may talk with you, as the peer counselor advisor, at any time about any person. This is so to avoid a situation where they are concerned about someone or their response to someone and yet cannot talk about it. Explain when they share confidential information with you, then you as a professional are bound by the rule of confidentiality.

Explain the other exception is any case where they know someone is suicidal or is being sexually or physically abused. In those cases, they *must* notify you! Confidentiality is intended to protect a person from harm. If a person is in a potentially life threatening situation, confidentiality no longer has meaning. Tell the peer counselors in those cases, you must follow your guidelines as a professional in reporting the situation to the appropriate authorities. Explain this is also a way to protect the peer counselors. By leaving them no room to decide whether to report a case, you have taken the responsibility for that decision off their shoulders.

Ask if the peer counselors have any questions on confidentiality or its exceptions. Ask them to give you several examples of what is, and what is not, a break in confidentiality as a way to assess and clarify their understanding.

Challenge:
Tell another student at our school how important confidentiality is to a peer counselor and what will happen if a break in confidentiality occurs.

Day 3.

Ask for discussion or questions on Challenges.

Display the poster listing the peer counselor "NORMS" in a prominent location in the classroom.

The peer counselor advisor begins the "What's My Bag" activity by going first. Continue to go-around the circle, having the peer counselors share their "bags."

Challenge:
Sit by a different person in here every day.

Day 4.

Ask for discussion or questions on Challenges.

Continue the "What's My Bag" activity until everyone has shared.

Process:
Who did you feel was especially open and honest during this activity?

Whose "bag" surprised you the most?

Is there something your would like to ask about a person's "bag?"

Is there anything you would like to add to your "bag?"

Challenge:
Tell a family member, preferably the one you usually share with the least, about something you have inside your "bag."

Day 5.

Ask for discussion or questions on Challenges.

Introduce the next activity with a statement such as the following: "We are going to look at the ways we limit ourselves and others by how we *label* ourselves and others. In a moment, I am going to ask for six volunteers who will sit in front of the group. These six volunteers are going to discuss a topic which I will give them. However, the 'catch' is the volunteers are going to wear labels. Others will react to what a person's label says rather than to what that person says."

Ask for six volunteers. Arrange the volunteers in a semi-circle so they can see each other and so the other peer counselors can see them. Put a hat or headband with one of the following messages on each volunteer: AGREE WITH ME, DISAGREE WITH ME, IGNORE ME, RIDICULE EVERYTHING I SAY, BE CONFUSED BY WHAT I SAY, ASK MY OPINION. As much as possible, choose a label different from the way people usually respond to the volunteer. Make sure the volunteers can see each other's labels without being able to see their own.

Give the volunteers a controversial topic to discuss, such as any recent change in school policy or a local or national current event. Their goal is to come up with a solution to the situation. During the discussion, they are to respond the way a person's *label says* rather than to what the *person says.*

Begin the discussion by asking the person with the label "AGREE WITH ME" to begin. After about five minutes call time.

Process:
Have the volunteers guess what their label says. Ask them to share their feelings during this activity.

Ask the observers to comment on what happened during this activity.

What are some additional examples of ways we label others and ourselves?

What are some of the "groups," or cliques, in the school. What are some of the ways they are "labeled?"

Challenge:
Identify someone in your life you have "labeled." Approach that person with respect and acceptance. Observe the reaction.

(NOTE: Set a date for collecting Challenges, if you are collecting them after every fifth Challenge. Respond to the experiences described on the peer counselors' Challenge Reports by offering suggestions, encouragement, a different perspective, or an acknowledgment of their strengths.)

As an optional activity, ask the peer counselors if they would like to have secret pals within the group, or "secret peers." If so, have each person, including the peer counselor advisor, write the following kinds of information on identical pieces of paper: name, address, phone number, locker number, birth date, favorite color, hobbies or interests, favorite food, favorite musical group, and their "certain something." A "certain something" is the thing they particularly enjoy having people do for them or give them. Examples of "certain somethings" are humorous cards, stuffed animals, a single flower, freshly baked cookies, posters with a message, a hug when they are down, or a smile and a happy greeting.

Have everyone fold their pieces of paper in the same way and put them all in a container. Have the peer counselors draw the name of their "secret peer."

Day 6.

Ask for discussion or questions on Challenges.

Describe the new student buddy program to the peer counselors. Explain it is designed to give new students someone they can talk to and to insure someone will know if a new student is having serious problems. Explain many times when people move during the school year, it is because of problems in the family, such as divorce, a change in custody, or a parent losing a job. Point out it is difficult enough moving to a new school without dealing with the other changes that are often occurring in the family.

Explain after a new student registers, the counseling secretary will show the new student a list of the peer counselors. This list will include a description of the peer counselors, which they will write in a few minutes. New students get to *select* the peer counselor who will welcome them. Then the counseling secretary sends for the peer counselor, writing the words "new student" on the request. Explain the peer counselors are to welcome the new students, show them around the school, locate their lockers, help them get their ID cards and library cards, and so forth. In addition, the peer counselors and their new students are to trade schedules so they know how to find each other and to make plans to meet for lunch the first day. It often works well for peer counselors and their new students to meet as a group for lunch as a way of introducing new students to each other. The peer counselors also ask about the interests of the new students and describe the clubs and activities that are available in the school.

Tell the peer counselors you are going to do an activity to focus on how it feels to be a new student. This activity will also help them look at what works and what doesn't work in the welcoming process. Have the group pick one of the peer counselors to be a new student. No one may volunteer, and the group picks the new student in any way they wish. The "new student" leaves the room while the rest of the peer counselors decide what setting they will use, such as the school cafeteria. They also decide which person will be the "peer counselor" to greet the "new student." The peer counselors divide up into several small groups, and the small groups each decide how they will greet the "new student." After everyone is ready, the "peer counselor" welcomes the "new student" and makes introductions to the others.

Process:
Ask the "new student" to talk about how it felt being chosen as the "new student" and also how it felt being introduced to the small groups.

Ask the "new student" to identify the things people did to create the most welcome, and most uncomfortable, feelings.

Ask the entire group to identify the different ways they saw the "new student" being greeted. Is this the way it is for new students at this school?

Are there any special problems new students will experience here?

Have any of you moved recently? How did you feel? What were some of the things people did that made you feel welcome? What were some ways you found to become part of the school?

Have the peer counselors write a short description of themselves which includes some of their interests and activities. Have them identify the class periods they can afford to miss occasionally to welcome a new student. Tell the peer counselors you will put the descriptions together in a list, like the one located in the Appendix, and the list will be posted by the counseling secretary's desk.

Challenge:
Explain the new student buddy program to each teacher whose class you may occasionally miss to welcome a new student.

Day 7.

Ask for discussion or questions on Challenges.

Tell the peer counselors you are beginning actual training today. Do an overview for them of all that their training will include. Emphasize being *chosen* as a peer counselor is the first step in *becoming* a peer counselor. The final step in becoming a peer counselor occurs when they have successfully completed training. Explain because of the importance of the work they will do, you can allow only those who demonstrate the characteristics of helping people to work as peer counselors. Explain their commitment, involvement, and progress during training will determine whether they actually *become* peer counselors.

Have the peer counselors read "Pitfalls on the Path to Helping" and "Do You 'Should' on Yourself? (Or Others?)," writing down their reactions, questions, and any personal examples as they read.

Process:
Which "pitfall" surprised you the most?

Which topic will help you the most personally?

What questions do you have on any topic?

Do you have any personal examples of these topics you would like to share?

Have the peer counselors form dyads to complete the following Challenge:

Challenge:
Decide which "pitfall" will be the hardest for you to avoid. Talk to another peer counselor about your feelings and experiences with this "pitfall." Decide how you will respond in the future.

Skills Development (Day 8-28)

Day 8.

Ask for discussion or questions on Challenges.

Have the peer counselors complete the "Peer Helping Pre-Test." Explain after their training is finished, they will complete the identical test as a post-test. Emphasize the pre- and post-tests are used only to show their growth and development in helping skills. Collect the pre-tests and save them for comparison with the post-tests.

Have the peer counselors read and discuss "Rules of Brainstorming."

Tell the peer counselors you are going to be discussing the different ways people communicate. Make the following statement: "All of you communicate all of the time!" Ask if there is anyone who *doesn't* communicate all of the time. (You will usually get at least one person who claims not to communicate. If not, say something like, "So your parents would tell me you communicate with them all of the time?") Tell the people who say they don't communicate all the time you want them to demonstrate *not communicating*, since they have obviously gotten good at it.

At your signal, tell these people *not to communicate!* After a couple minutes, thank the peer counselors doing the demonstration and ask the other peer counselors if the "demonstrators" communicated any messages. As you list all the different messages people got, make the point we *do* all communicate all of the time. The message people get is not always what we think they will get or what we mean. If we want to improve our communication, we must become aware of the ways we communicate non-verbally, through our body language, as well as the ways we communicate verbally.

Non-Verbal Activity:
Have the peer counselors stand and begin walking around the room. Tell them to picture the others as hostile and have them respond non-verbally. (Allow about one

minute.) Now tell them to picture the group as completely accepting and again have them respond non-verbally. (Allow about one minute.)

After the peer counselors are seated again, have them brainstorm examples of non-verbal communication, including those they saw during the activity. For example, how do you know how your parents feel the minute they get home from work or how your friends feel the minute you see them?

Process:
What are some examples of non-verbal communication which are often misunderstood by others? (For example, being quiet is often mistaken for being aloof or "stuck-up." Or, when people are depressed, others often think they are angry.)

Explain sometimes people's verbal and non-verbal communications don't match. Ask the peer counselors to give examples of this. (For example, people say they are fine, but they look or sound depressed. Or people say they are angry, but they are smiling.) Make the point in these cases, it is the *non-verbal* communication people believe!

Challenge:
In the next 24 hours, list all the ways you communicate non-verbally. Put a star next to the ones which other people could easily misunderstand.

Day 9.

Ask for discussion or questions on Challenges.

Ask the peer counselors to turn to the "Attending Skill" in their manual. However, before they begin reading, have them find a page nearby with room for them to write. Tell them when you give the signal, you want them to write this statement as fast as they can three times: "I am working to be the best peer counselor I can be." Give the signal. As soon as everyone has finished, tell them now you want them to *switch hands* and do the same thing! Again give the signal.

Process:
Compare observations during this activity.

What made the two parts of this activity different, since it involved doing the same process twice?

Emphasize the only difference is they have practiced and become comfortable with one hand, and they have not done that with the other hand. With an equal amount of time given to practicing with both hands, most people could write equally well with either hand if it was important to them. Explain this is true with any new skill we learn. Until we have practiced enough for it to become a natural response, we feel awkward and uncomfortable. This is particularly true as we try new ways of relating to others. At first the focus is on the new skill we are learning, and our responses may feel programmed or phony. As we continue to use the new skill, we begin to incorporate it into our own personality. Then it simply becomes one of the ways we respond to others. Tell the peer counselors you hope they will remember this whenever they happen to notice these sentences written in their manual.

Have the peer counselors read and discuss "Attending Skill."

If you have advanced peer counselors, have them model the attending skill by doing a demonstration of the skill in action. If not, ask for a volunteer and model the attending skill for the peer counselors. Discuss.

Tell the peer counselors they are going to do an activity to practice using attending skills. Have the peer counselors form dyads, getting with someone they do not know as well as the others. Have them decide who will be the "speaker" and who will be the "listener" for this activity. Have copies made of the "Non-Attending Activity," located in the Appendix. Give a copy of the speaker's instructions to one person in each dyad and a copy of the listener's instructions to the other person in the dyad. Tell the peer counselors to begin as soon as they have read their instructions.

After a few minutes say, "Stop, please!" (You may need to repeat this two or three times depending on how involved they are with each other.) Ask the listeners and speakers to show their instructions to each other.

Process:

Ask the speakers to talk about how they felt during this activity.

Also ask the listeners to talk about how they felt while they were using non-attending behaviors.

Have the peer counselors stay in the same dyads. This time have them switch roles so the speakers become the listeners. Have the speakers follow the same instructions, but this time the listeners are to demonstrate effective attending skills. Allow five to ten minutes for this.

Have the peer counselors read "Please Hear What I'm Not Saying." After they have finished, ask them to think of someone this poem describes. Give them the following Challenge:

Challenge:

In a conversation, completely attend to the person you thought of when you read "Please Hear What I'm Not Saying."

Day 10.

Ask for discussion or questions on Challenges.

Introduce the concept of the training triad. Explain to the peer counselors a training triad consists of a "helper," a "friend," and an "observer." Training triads will be used at the completion of each skill.

The "helpers" are the people taking the role of peer counselors. They will be practicing the skill just learned, as well as all previous skills.

The "friends" are the people talking. They may choose to talk about personal issues or to role play a situation. Explain to the peer counselors you have role play topics they may use for this. At the end of the training triad session, the friend may offer feedback to the helper on what was especially effective or distracting.

The "observers" do not verbally participate in the session in any way. They observe the helper, making notes on the Skills Chart. In using the Skills Chart, the observers make a check mark in one of the boxes next to a behavior each time the behavior is demonstrated. In this way the observers develop a profile for the helpers of all the behaviors demonstrated and how often they occur. This allows the helpers to see areas of strength and areas being omitted. The observers do *not evaluate* the helpers. Instead, they make observations, or they may offer feedback to the helper by discussing what they would have felt in the position of friend. It is important the observers stay in their role until the session is finished. If there is something the observers wanted to say during the conversation, they may talk about that when the session is finished.

Explain after the friend finishes talking and the helper has received the Skills Chart and any feedback, each person changes roles within the training triad. After the second session is completed, each person changes roles again. In this way each person experiences each role within the training triad.

After explaining training triads, do a demonstration of a training triad for the peer counselors. Have a copy of the "Role Play Topics for Training Triads," located in the Appendix, cut apart and placed in an envelope to offer to the friends in the training triads.

Form training triads, using the Skills Chart to the Attending Skill.

After each person has experienced each role within the training triad, have the peer counselors come back to the main circle. "Do Acknowledgments" of the special things you saw happening while they were in their training triads. Ask if any of the peer counselors have any acknowledgments they would like to do also.

Day 11.

Have the peer counselors read and discuss "Empathy Skill."

Have advanced peer counselors model this skill by doing a demonstration of the skill in action. Or, ask for a volunteer and model the empathy skill for the peer counselors. Discuss.

Explain to the peer counselors in developing our ability to understand people and what they are experiencing, we must learn to listen effectively. Most people think there isn't much skill involved in listening. They tend to confuse *hearing* with listening. However, without developing some tools for effective listening, most people miss a great deal of what others say to them.

Tell the peer counselors you are going to do an activity to practice listening effectively. Ask for two volunteers. One person will take the role of a person named "Brian," and the other will take the role of the "peer counselor." Ask both of them to stand with you in front of the group. Explain you are going to introduce Brian to the peer counselor by reading "Brian's Story," located in the Appendix. After you have finished reading the story, the peer counselor will introduce Brian to the group by repeating Brian's story.

Process:
Ask "Brian" and the "peer counselor" how they felt during this activity.

Ask the "peer counselor" if being in front of the group interfered with being able to listen effectively. Make the point nervousness about how we are "performing" will always interfere with our ability to listen effectively.

Identify the information from "Brian's Story" that was included and omitted when he was "introduced" to the group.

What are some of the feelings you would guess Brian might have?

Have the peer counselors read and discuss "Becoming an Active Listener" and "Listen."

Challenge:
After a conversation on a personal topic with a friend or family member, identify the significant facts, main themes, and the feelings of the person speaking.

Day 12.

Ask for discussion and questions on Challenges.

Explain to the peer counselors part of the skill of effective listening is learning how to *show* people we have heard and understood what they said.

Have the peer counselors complete Part I of "Reflection of Feelings and Content." Compare and discuss the different possible responses.

Have the peer counselors complete Part II of "Reflection of Feelings and Content." Compare and discuss the different possible responses.

Have the peer counselors complete PART III of "Reflection of Feelings and Content." Ask for volunteers to role play the person talking in each situation, with other peer counselors verbally giving the responses they have written. Do examples of different responses to situations. There are rarely "right" and "wrong" responses to situations. Compare the different responses, focusing on the possible *effects* of each response.

In order to practice using empathy responses in a conversation, do "A Student's Saga" as a group. Ask one of the peer counselors to role play the student speaking, while the others make responses. Compare possible responses and their likely effects.

Challenge:
Use Empathy Skill (reflection of feelings and content) in five conversations before our next class.

Day 13.

Ask for discussion or questions on Challenges.

Tell the peer counselors you will be doing training triads again the next day. Explain they will still be able to use role play topics if they choose. It is much easier for the helper to practice skills when the friend talks about actual personal issues. As the helper, it is difficult to really get into the feelings of a situation when you know a person is only pretending to have a problem.

Explain training triads are also an opportunity for the peer counselors to deal with some of their own feelings about situations in their lives. Being open about our feelings and situations is called self-disclosure. Self-disclosure is sometimes difficult for people because they are embarrassed by what they see as failures or weaknesses. They have forgotten other people often have similar feelings.

Tell the peer counselors you are going to do an activity designed to help work through any feelings of this kind within the group. Hand out identically sized pieces of paper. Have the peer counselors list three failures, deficiencies, faults, or situations about which they are embarrassed or ashamed. Tell them to write their responses in block printing, although no attempt will be made to identify the writer.

Collect the pieces of paper and shuffle them. Ask one of the peer counselors to write the responses on a chalkboard or large pad of paper as you read them. If some responses are repeated, mark the frequencies.

Process:
How do you feel after doing this activity?

Comment everyone was able to identify "faults" or problem situations in their lives. This is why it is easier for other people to identify with our feelings than we think they will. They often have similar feelings themselves. The more we can be open about our own feelings, the easier we make it for others to do the same. Most of us feel extremely vulnerable when we disclose the things we see as inadequacies in ourselves. Ironically, though, people are more likely to care about us and feel close to us when they understand our feelings and experiences than when they see only the "face" we choose to wear.

Ask the peer counselors to do "An Exercise in Self-Disclosure." Explain this is an opportunity for them to identify parts of their personalities or aspects of their lives they would like to change. If they choose, they may talk about some of these issues during training triads, rather than relying on role play topics.

Challenge:
In the next three days, talk to a trusted friend, family member, or peer counselor about one of the issues you identified in "An Exercise in Self-Disclosure."

Day 14.

Ask for discussion or questions on Challenges.

Before beginning training triads, explain to the peer counselors the skills they are learning are in the order they will generally be used in a helping relationship. By focusing on using the skills in this order, they can better provide an opportunity for awareness and growth for the person talking with them. Although it is natural for the peer counselors to focus on the most recent skill in a training triad session, it is important for them to always "begin at the beginning" with the Attending Skill.

Form training triads, using the Skills Chart to the Empathy Skill.

Do Acknowledgments

Day 15.

Have the peer counselors read and discuss "Clarifying/Questioning Skill" and "Some Clarifying Questions."

Have advanced peer counselors model this skill by doing a demonstration of the skill in action. Or, ask for a volunteer and model the clarifying/questioning skill for the peer counselors. Discuss.

Have the peer counselors form dyads, getting with someone they haven't worked with or still don't know as well as the others. Their task is to discover their partner's (1) deepest values, (2) greatest dreams, and (3) happiest moments. However, they may *only ask closed questions!* The peer counselors each have three minutes to question their partners.

Process:
How did you feel while being asked so many closed questions?

How did you feel while you were the one asking the closed questions?

Did anyone feel prejudged by the questions?

Staying in the same dyads, the peer counselors are again to discover their partner's (1) deepest values, (2) greatest dreams, and (3) happiest moments. This time they may use open and clarifying questions. They again each have three minutes to question their partners.

When time is called, have the peer counselors return to the large circle and share what they learned about their partner with the entire group.

Challenge:
Ask an open question of a stranger, a student you do not know, the teacher you know the least about, and a parent when you do not already know the answer.

Day 16.
Ask for discussion or questions on Challenges.

Form training triads, using the Skills Chart to the Clarifying/Questioning Skill. Do Acknowledgments

Day 17.
Have the peer counselors read and discuss "Assertiveness Skill."

Have them complete "Assess Your Assertiveness" as a way to rate their assertiveness level. Discuss the reasons for subtracting some responses from the total score.

Have advanced peer counselors model assertiveness by using "I" messages in several different role play situations. Or, ask for volunteers and do this demonstration for the peer counselors. Discuss.

Challenge:
Identify an area of your life in which you would like to respond more assertively. Talk to a friend, family member, or peer counselor about this situation.

Day 18.

Ask for discussion or questions on Challenges.

Tell the peer counselors you are going to do an activity to introduce the concept of "You" messages. On a chalkboard or large pad of paper, write examples of several "You" message sentence stems, such as:

"You are...."
"You have...."
"You would...."
"You should...."

Give examples of each of these, such as :

"You are so pretty."
"You have such big feet."
"You *would* be the one to drop the milk."
"You should be grateful for all I have done for you."

Have the peer counselors brainstorm all the "You" messages they have heard from people. The "You" messages may be negative or positive. After time has been called, have the peer counselors choose the "You" message they identify with most closely.

Explain to the peer counselors after all the instructions are given, they will stand and begin walking around the room. As they approach another peer counselor, they are to stop, shake hands, and introduce themselves with their "You" message. However, they are now to phrase their "You" message in the form of an "I" message! For example, "Hi! My name is Carol, and I am such a troublemaker." My partner might respond by saying, "Hi! My name is Tim, and I should be more considerate." After demonstrating the process, have the peer counselors stand and begin.

Process:
How did you feel introducing yourself *as* your "You" message?

Is this something people tend to do unconsciously?

What is the effect of a "You" message?

Explain self-fulfilling prophecy and ask how it relates to "You" messages. (For example, if people have heard all their lives they are clumsy, they will usually think of themselves as clumsy and *become even clumsier*.) Emphasize we all tend to internalize what other people say about us, especially when we are young. This is part of what determines how we see ourselves and what we learn to expect of ourselves.

Have the peer counselors complete PART I of "'I' Messages: Learning to Speak Assertively." Compare and discuss possible responses.

Have the peer counselors complete PART II of "'I' Messages: Learning to Speak Assertively." Compare and discuss possible responses and the likely effect of each response.

Have the peer counselors complete PART III of "'I' Messages: Learning to Speak Assertively." Ask for volunteers to role play situations, with other peer counselors verbally giving their "You" message and then their "I" message responses.

Challenge:
Use an "I" message with someone with whom you are having difficulty communicating.

Day 19.

Ask for discussion or questions on Challenges.

Have the peer counselors read and discuss "Styles of Interaction: Passive, Assertive, and Aggressive" and "The Body Language of Assertive Behavior."

Have advanced peer counselors do a demonstration in which they respond to the same situation passively, aggressively, and then assertively. Or, ask for a volunteer and do this demonstration for the peer counselors. Discuss.

Have the peer counselors brainstorm examples of situations in which they have difficulty saying no or in which they feel peer pressure. For example, someone asks to borrow your car, and you don't want to lend it to them. Or, you are at a party where things start happening you don't like, but you feel pressured to go along. Make a list of all the examples identified.

Have the peer counselors form small groups of three or four. Explain they are each to identify a situation from the list in which they have difficulty responding assertively. They are to explain the situation to the others in their group and to explain what role the others are to play. They are to role play each situation three times giving a passive response, next an aggressive response, and last an assertive response.

Process:
Ask the peer counselors which response seemed most natural and comfortable for them. Explain this is probably their normal style of response.

How did you feel using each response?

What are some of the reactions you got with each type of response?

What are some of the things people will do when others are assertive, and they don't like it?

What are some ways to handle this?

Have the peer counselors do "An Exercise in Developing Assertiveness."

Challenge:
In the next 24 hours, rate each one of your responses as passive, aggressive, or assertive.

Day 20.

Ask for discussion or questions on Challenges.

Clarify the difference between a "You" message and a statement that is a reflection of feelings, such as "You are beginning to feel frustrated with her." Make the point a "You" message is something *we* put on another person. When we reflect feelings, we mirror back to people what *they* have communicated they are feeling.

Form training triads, using the Skills Chart to the Assertiveness Skill.

Do Acknowledgments

Day 21.

Having arranged this a few days earlier, have a "confrontation" between two of the advanced peer counselors erupt at the start of class. Or, privately make arrangements with one of the peer counselors to have this "confrontation" with you. The confrontation is to be one which violates all of the guidelines of an effective confrontation.

Process:
After explaining this was only a demonstration, ask how everyone was feeling during the "confrontation."

How many of you have had experiences just like this that make you uncomfortable with the idea of confrontation?

Have the peer counselors identify everything that went wrong during the "confrontation."

Make the point this "confrontation" was really a "blow-up," rather than an effective confrontation.

Have the peer counselors read and discuss "Confrontation Skill" and "I Will Do You No Favor."

Have the peer counselors read and discuss "Rules for Fighting Fair: Because All is NOT Fair in Love and War."

Have advanced peer counselors model effective confrontation skills in a demonstration. Or, ask for a volunteer and do this demonstration for the peer counselors. Discuss.

Ask the peer counselors to brainstorm a list of conflicts they have with family or friends. Have the peer counselors each pick a conflict they have difficulty handling effectively. Then have the peer counselors form triads. One peer counselor takes the role of the person with whom there is a conflict. Another peer counselor uses effective confrontation skills to find a positive solution with this person. The third peer counselor takes the role of observer, offering feedback after the demonstration. Have the peer counselors switch roles until they have each had an opportunity to practice using effective confrontation skills.

Choose some of these solutions to demonstrate before the entire group.

Process:
What is the most difficult part of confrontation for you?

What are some of your fears about confrontation?

What are the some of the benefits of learning to use confrontation effectively?

Challenge:
Identify the "rule for fighting fair" you break most often. In the next three days, keep track of how often you violate this rule.

Day 22.

Ask for discussion or questions on Challenges.

Have the peer counselors complete "Helper Confrontation." Compare different responses and their likely effects. Ask for volunteers to role play situations, giving the passive, aggressive, and assertive ways they confront themselves or others.

Challenge:
Confront a friend, teacher, parent, or employer with a feeling or concern you have never expressed.

Day 23.

Ask for discussion or questions on Challenges.

Form training triads, using the Skills Chart to the Confrontation Skill.

Do Acknowledgments

Day 24.

Have the peer counselors read and discuss "Problem-Solving Skill."

Have advanced peer counselors do a demonstration of this skill in action. Or, ask for a volunteer and demonstrate this skill for the peer counselors. Discuss.

Explain to the peer counselors one of the most important steps in problem-solving is for people to know what is most important to them. Any plan of action must be evaluated in light of a person's values.

Have the peer counselors complete "Personal Priorities."

Process:
Have the peer counselors check their prioritizing by asking themselves how they would feel if they never experienced the last three items in their priority rating.

Would your best friend already know how you feel about your top three items?

During problem-solving it is often difficult for people to recognize their choices. People often approach their lives as if they only have two choices: yes/no, always/never, either/or, and so on. They often ignore all of their other options.

For each issue described below, draw a line on a chalkboard with the extreme (either/or) choices at each end of the line. When the peer counselors identify other alternatives to the situation, have them write their alternative where they feel it belongs on the line. After everyone has had an opportunity to respond, have the peer counselors consider each alternative and predict its likely consequences.

ISSUE: Other students constantly hassle you, and you are sick of it. What do you do?

Beat them up	Pretend you don't notice

ISSUE: Your parents have set a curfew for you two hours earlier than what you think is reasonable. What do you do?

Come in whenever you like	Refuse to go out at all

ISSUE: As a parent, your son or daughter is picked up for drunk driving. What do you do?

Say: "Don't come home."   Say:"Kids will be kids"

Challenge:

List all of the examples of "either/or" thinking you hear in the next three days, including your own.

Day 25.

Ask for discussion or questions on Challenges.

Have the peer counselors read and discuss "No-Lose Problem-Solving: Life Doesn't have to be a No-Win or Win-Lose Proposition."

Have advanced peer counselors demonstrate a no-lose solution to a situation. Or, ask for a volunteer and demonstrate a no-lose solution for the following situation:

> Person A and Person B are college roommates.

> Person A: Your friend, George, has made a piece of art (junk sculpture) just for you, and you *really* like it! It means a lot to you to receive this gift from George, and you want to display it in a prominent place in your apartment. You think the living room would be the perfect place!

> Person B: You *hate* that piece of junk George calls art! The color, design, and style will not fit in your already overcrowded living room. What's more, you don't particularly like George. He has always treated you like a piece of furniture!

Process:

What did you observe during this demonstration?

What message, besides what was being said, did you hear in the conversation?

Would you have done anything differently?

Another important part of problem-solving is knowing what you want and deciding how you plan to get it. Have the peer counselors read and discuss "Goals: Because If You Don't Know Where You Are Going, You Will Undoubtedly End Up Somewhere Else."

Challenge:
Develop a goal statement for yourself.

Day 26.

Ask for discussion or questions on Challenges.

Form training triads, using the Skills Chart to the Problem-Solving Skill.

Do Acknowledgments

Day 27.

Preparation for the "Peer Helping Skills Exam."

Explain to the peer counselors the skills exam is not designed to "catch" them not knowing something. Rather, it is an opportunity for them to review what they have learned about each skill in order to better incorporate it into their lives. Tell the peer counselors they will each receive an "A" on this exam. If any peer counselors do not fully cover a skill on the exam, you will have them rewrite the skill. However, before rewriting it, the peer counselors will review the material on the skill again, and they will either talk with you or with one other peer counselor about the skill. This process will be repeated until every peer counselor has demonstrated a superior understanding of the use and value of every skill.

Help the peer counselors review for the "Peer Helping Skills Exam" by covering the key points of each skill.

Day 28.

Have the peer counselors complete the "Peer Helping Skills Exam."

Topic Development (Day 29-50)

Day 29.

Suicide Prevention and Intervention.

Idealistically, the best time to train the peer counselors for suicide prevention and intervention is after they have completed their skills training. Realistically, however, you may find that due to the environment in your school or community, you cannot safely wait that long. If that is your situation, the peer counselors can be effectively trained in suicide prevention and intervention much earlier in the program. In this case, tell the peer counselors early in the training when you will begin this unit. I have found this to be important in allowing the peer counselors to become mentally prepared for the subject, *especially* if there have been recent suicides in the school or community. The suicide prevention and intervention unit would then begin on Day 8, after the peer counselors complete the "Peer Helping Pre-Test."

Have the peer counselors complete "Suicide: Myths or Facts?" and then read "Suicide: The Facts."

Have the peer counselors read "Suicide: The Ultimate Tragedy."

Process:
Ask the peer counselors to talk about any experiences they have had that make this topic a difficult one.

Ask the peer counselors how they feel about being required to report to you, or others you designate, when they know someone who is talking about suicide or showing other warning signs. Emphasize the reason for this policy is to prevent any situation in which they might feel responsible if others attempt or commit suicide.

Talk to the peer counselors about the fears people have of "looking silly" if they report a situation, and it turns out to be "nothing." Explain people who find themselves in that situation have still done something extremely important.

They have clearly communicated their belief in the importance of another person's life and well-being.

Ask the peer counselors if they know someone who is always talking about suicide. Explain the needs of a person doing this and talk to them about ways to handle it. Make sure the peer counselors understand they are always to take this person seriously and to continue to report the situation each time it occurs.

Day 30.

At the same time we are experiencing an epidemic of suicidal behavior by young people, there are also many students who have no understanding, and sometimes no empathy, for those who become suicidal. While inappropriate attention for suicidal behavior is not helpful, appropriate attention in the form of recognition and referral is absolutely critical. Appropriate attention results from an understanding of the basis for suicidal feelings.

In order to help the peer counselors understand the layer upon layer of events and feelings involved when people become suicidal, demonstrate the "Last Straw Event," taken from *Preventing Teenage Suicide: The Living Alternative Handbook* by Polly Joan, Human Sciences Press, Inc. and used with permission.

Last Straw Event

Begin this demonstration by drawing an unhappy Karen stick figure on a chalkboard or large pad of paper. Say: "As so many people do during their teenage years, Karen feels ugly, confused, lonely, and worthless." Write the words ugly, confused, lonely, and worthless next to the Karen stick figure.

First Layer:

Say: "However, on top of these feelings, Karen's parents have recently gotten a divorce." Draw the first layer over Karen and write: "parents get a divorce." Ask the peer counselors how Karen might be feeling as a result of the divorce. Write their responses on the same layer. They will include feelings such as guilty, rejected, conflict, anger, loss, and hurting.

Second Layer:

Say: "Since what happens to people at home usually affects how they are at school, Karen acts depressed at school most of the time." Draw the second layer over Karen and write: "depressed." Say: "Since Karen is depressed so often, after awhile her friends start to back off." Write: "friends back off" on the same layer. Ask the peer counselors how Karen probably feels now. Their responses will include feelings such as rejected, isolated, loss, hurting, and lonely. Write them on the same layer.

Third Layer:

Say: "When someone is really depressed, it is almost impossible to concentrate or study." Draw the third layer over Karen and write: "hard to study." Say: "And when it's hard to study, the next thing that usually happens is grades go down." Write: "grades go down" on the same layer. Ask the peer counselors how Karen probably feels now, and write their responses on the same layer. They will include feelings such as failure, rejection, worthlessness, anxiety, and stress.

Fourth Layer:

Say: "The situation for Karen just seems to get worse and worse, with one problem on top of another. She's starting to feel hopeless. But one thing Karen still has going for her is her pride at being on the swimming team. However, because Karen has been so depressed, she has missed a lot of practice. She also hasn't worked very hard during the practices she has attended. The next thing that happens is Karen is dropped from the swimming team." Draw the fourth layer over Karen and write: "kicked off the swim team." Say: "And this may be the *last straw* for Karen."

Your final picture will look like this:

Process:

Is it possible Karen might attempt suicide?

What are some of the things Karen might be saying? (For example: What's the use? Nothing works out anymore! It's hopeless! What is there to live for? I've lost everything!)

If Karen tries to kill herself, will it be because she got kicked off the swimming team?

What are some things other people could have done to help Karen?

Do you know anyone who reminds you of Karen?

Day 31.

Have the peer counselors read and discuss "Techniques of Assessment and Intervention."

"Contract" is one of the components of intervention. Explain to the peer counselors contracting is one of the most powerful tools for working with suicidal people. In a 1973 study conducted by Drye, Goulding, and Goulding, there were no fatalities out of 609 cases when no-suicide contracts were used. Also, students will often view a contract with another student as being even more binding than with an adult. However, the use of the no-suicide contract is *always* followed by an immediate referral to a counselor. When a person will not contract, this often weighs heavily in a decision to hospitalize.

Have the peer counselors read and discuss "No-Suicide Contract" and "Levels of Suicidal Risk."

Be prepared at this time to explain to the peer counselors:

- the system of referral within your school,
- your school's crisis response team members,
- your school's crisis response plan, and
- the peer counselors' role and responsibility.

An excellent source for developing a school crisis response plan is *Responding To Student Suicide: The First 48 Hours,* available for $2.00 from Phi Delta Kappa International, P.O. Box 789, Bloomington, IN 47402-0789.

Day 32.

Ask peer counselors who have known students who were suicidal to volunteer to role play the situations. The peer counselor advisor takes the role of the peer counselor, giving a demonstration of assessment and intervention. Do as many role plays as possible.

Use these role plays to clarify the peer counselors' understanding of assessment and intervention techniques and their responses in different types of situations.

Day 33.

As most people have experienced, the most severe crises have a way of developing in the evenings, on weekends, and during holidays. It is critically important for the peer counselor advisor to establish a network among members of the community, so there is *always* a place where students can get help.

Students will not usually refer to an agency or to a person they do not know. In order to build a bridge between the school and the community, invite the director of your community crisis intervention program to talk to the peer counselors. Ask the director to explain the community program and to talk about how interventions are handled. Be sure the peer counselors know specifically *how* they make contact with someone in this program and precisely *what* they can expect as a result of the referral.

Day 34.

Pass around a piece of school stationery, and ask the peer counselors to each write a short "Thank You" to your guest speaker. Do this each time someone visits your group.

Alcoholism

Have the peer counselors read and discuss "Alcoholism" and "But He (or She) Doesn't *Look* Like an Alcoholic."

To help the peer counselors better understand and experience the survival roles within a chemically dependent family, do the following demonstration:

Sculpture of a Chemically Dependent Family

This demonstration is based on a technique called family sculpturing, originated by Virginia Satir. In family sculpturing, people "draw" a picture of their family by posing and positioning all the family members as they see them. However, in this demonstration, rather than focusing on a particular family, the focus is on the alcoholic family and on the survival roles that develop within that family. Sharon Wegscheider identified these roles in her book, *Another Chance: Hope and Health for the Alcoholic Family.*

Ask for a volunteer to take the role of "dependent." Ask the dependent to name the drug of choice and to stand on a chair to represent the crutch of the drug. The dependent is to stay focused on a point high on the opposite wall where there is an unending supply of the drug. This represents the dependent's increasing preoccupation with the drug and also increasing withdrawal from the family. The dependent's feelings are anger because people don't understand, fear of discovery, and shame and remorse at a growing sense of worthlessness and loss of control. These feelings feed a growing depression which shows itself in loss of appetite, listlessness, and difficulty sleeping. The dependent progresses to angry, hostile behavior, projecting self-hate and blaming onto the family. Finally, the dependent retreats into coldness, seeming to have no feeling for the family at all.

Ask for a volunteer to take the role of "chief enabler," the dependent's spouse in this case. Instruct the chief enabler to stand facing the dependent. Instruct the dependent to lean on the chief enabler's shoulders, using the chief enabler for support. The chief enabler is a loving and loyal spouse but has been replaced by the dependent's love of the drug of choice. The chief enabler feels physical and emotional rejection by the dependent and ever increasing loneliness as other social contacts are dropped because of the dependent's unpredictability. Before long, the chief enabler is playing the part of both parents, making most of the family decisions, controlling the finances, and probably taking an extra job to earn more money. The chief enabler feels deep fear at the eventual consequences of the dependent's using. However, even though the load of the chief enabler is a heavy one, it also gives this person an opportunity to demonstrate a supreme competence and capability.

Ask for a volunteer to take the role of "hero." Instruct the hero to stand in front of the family, facing in the same direction as the dependent. This is the first born child who has learned to survive and to protect the family through super achievement. This child provides a screen to the world to prevent anyone from seeing the family for what it is. The hero has learned not to talk about negative feelings, to tell people what they want to hear, and to never talk to anyone about the dependent's using. Instruct the hero to keep looking back over a shoulder at the dependent and chief enabler.

Ask for a volunteer to take the role of "scapegoat." Instruct the scapegoat to stand off to one side with back turned to the rest of the family. The scapegoat is the hostile, rebellious second child. The scapegoat can't compete positively with the hero, so this person does it negatively by getting into trouble. The scapegoat eventually withdraws from the family, sometimes by running away but often by simply spending more and more time away from home. Eventually, if typical, the scapegoat will continue to withdraw and escape by turning to chemicals. Ask the scapegoat what feelings are held concerning the dependent and the hero. Ask the hero how one feels about the scapegoat. Instruct the dependent, chief enabler, and hero to all turn at the same time and point at the scapegoat saying, "If it wasn't for you, we'd be okay!"

Ask for a volunteer to take the role of "lost child." Ask the lost child to show where one fits in the family. This will be somewhere off to one side where no one will notice. The lost child is the quiet, withdrawn member of the family who is constantly plagued with loneliness. This child becomes "invisible" by simply seeming to fade into the background. The lost child will have lots of pets and books but no friends. This child is the student no one remembers, the one other students call a "Zero." This is the one child the family doesn't have to think about.

Ask for a volunteer to take the role of "mascot." Instruct the mascot to continually go up to every member of the family, being super cute and constantly trying to keep their attention. The mascot is the youngest child, the one who provides comic relief or diversion for the family. The mascot's fun and energy are refreshing, for awhile. The mascot is often "Daddy's" favorite but can also become extremely tiresome. This is the child who often gets medicated with Ridelin, or other drugs, for hyperactivity.

In our continuing scenario, what often happens next is the scapegoat gets "busted." The parents are called by the school or by juvenile authorities. Ask the chief enabler how one feels about this. Also ask the dependent how one feels. Both parents are asked to go in for a conference, but it is the chief enabler who goes. If the person the chief enabler talks to is knowledgeable about the disease of chemical dependency, this person may be able to get the chief enabler to the help of an organization such as Al-Anon. In Al-Anon, the chief enabler will learn to quit enabling. Instruct the chief enabler to step away from the dependent, withdrawing support. It is only at this point treatment for a family in terrible pain may begin.

Process:

Ask the peer counselors who took the roles of family members to talk about how they feel.

Ask what observations were made by the other peer counselors.

Explain to the peer counselors survival roles also occur in families that are highly dysfunctional even when there is no chemical use. People will often recognize themselves in these survival roles even though they do not live in a chemically dependent family.

Explain also people sometimes take more than one role in a family and people sometimes take different roles at different times in their lives.

Day 35.

Have the peer counselors complete "Alcoholism Always Gives Warning Signs: But Sometimes No One Listens."

Have the peer counselors read and discuss "Someone I Know Drinks Too Much: What Should I Do?" "Adolescent Alcoholism," and "The Excuses and the Realities of Adolescent Alcoholism."

Process:

Because drinking is so wide spread among high school students, you may experience some resistance to the topic of adolescent alcoholism. If any peer counselors had a substance problem at one time, ask in advance if they would be willing to talk about it. Or, invite other students who have gone through treatment to discuss it with the peer counselors.

Day 36.

Have the peer counselors read and discuss "Children of Alcoholics" and "Indications That a Child May Be Living with Family Alcoholism."

Invite a guest speaker from Alateen or from Al-Anon to talk to the peer counselors.

Day 37.

Invite a member of Alcoholics Anonymous to talk to the peer counselors.

Day 38.

Invite an alcoholism counselor to talk to the peer counselors. Ask this person to include information on the role of endorphins in chemical dependency as part of the presentation.

Day 39.

Grief

Have the peer counselors read and discuss "Grief."

Process:
Ask the peer counselors if any of them have had an experience in dealing with grief they would be willing to talk about.

What are some of the things you needed from others?

Did people seem to understand what you were feeling?

What are some of the things you learned to do in dealing with your grief?

What were some of the most helpful things people did?

Day 40.

Invite a counselor from the school or community who specializes in working with the grief process or with bereavement groups to talk to the peer counselors.

Day 41.

Rape

Have the peer counselors read and discuss "Rape."

Invite a counselor from your local women's shelter or one who specializes in working with rape trauma to talk to the peer counselors about stranger rape and date rape.

Day 42.

Families

Have the peer counselors read and discuss "Our Families, Our Selves."

To develop deeper or more positive ties between the peer counselors and their families, do one or more of the following activities:

Activity 1: Have the peer counselors develop a family tree. In stepfamilies, this family tree is necessarily more complex, so be prepared to assist with this.

Activity 2: Have the peer counselors develop a list of open questions to ask family members at mealtimes, while traveling, or during "family meetings." It is important questions be appropriate for all members of the family regardless of age. The list could include ones such as:

What was the most important thing someone said to you today?
What has been your saddest moment this week?
What was your most memorable birthday, and why?
What do you know about yourself today that you didn't realize last year at this time?
What is one personal skill you are trying to develop?
What personal belief has been most influential in your life?

Activity 3: Have the peer counselors develop "interview" questions to use with their parents. The interview could include such questions as:

How did your parents discipline you when you were young?
What was it like for you as a teenager?
In what ways are you similar to your parents and different from them?
What were your favorite times with your family?
What was it like economically in your family?
What was the hardest time for you with your family?
What was the most important thing you learned from your family?

Have the peer counselors either ask their parents to develop interview questions for them or have the peer counselors develop interview questions for their parents to use.

Activity 4: Have the peer counselors brainstorm examples of traditions in their families and things they value about their families. Then have the peer counselors individually develop their own statement of the traditions and characteristics they want to have in their own families some day.

Day 43.

Divorce

Have the peer counselors read and discuss "Divorce: The Disintegration of a Family."

Process:

Ask the peer counselors whose families have gone through a divorce to talk about their needs at different ages and at the different stages of the divorce.

What made the divorce hardest?

In what ways have you grown as a result of the divorce?

What are some of the ways you have learned to integrate the divorce into your lives?

Day 44.

Stepfamilies

Have the peer counselors read and discuss "Stepfamilies: Families Learning to Walk in Step."

Invite a counselor who specializes in working with stepfamilies to talk to the peer counselors.

Day 45.

Dreams

Have the peer counselors read and discuss "Dreams: The Mirror of Your Mind."

Ask the peer counselors to talk about a recent dream, a recurring dream, or a particularly memorable dream.

Process:

What would you guess is the general message of your dream?

What significant events happened within two or three days of the dream?

What areas of your life or what relationship does your dream focus upon?

Is there a literal meaning to your dream?

What is the setting of your dream? What happens in places such as this?

Who are the people in your dream? What are they like? How do you feel about them? What is your relationship with them?

Can you feel the part of you that is like these people?

What are the objects in your dream?

What is the major action in the dream? What does it remind you of in your life?

How do you feel in the dream? What do the feelings in your dream remind you of in your life?

Provide a list for the peer counselors of books in the school library and the public library on the topic of dreams. Or, invite someone who specializes in dream study to talk to the peer counselors.

Day 46.

Teenage Pregnancy and AIDS

Invite someone from your county health clinic or from Planned Parenthood to talk to the peer counselors about teenage pregnancy and AIDS.

Day 47.

Eating Disorders

Invite a counselor who specializes in working with people who have eating disorders to talk to the peer counselors.

Day 48.

Family Violence

Invite the director of your local child protective services to talk to the peer counselors about the cycle of violence and family violence, including child abuse. Ask the director to talk about abuse reporting laws and the system for reporting abuse that exists between the schools and child protective services.

Day 49.

Stress Management

Invite a local authority on stress management to talk to the peer counselors.

Day 50.

Have the peer counselors take the "Peer Helping Post-Test." Return their copy of the "Peer Helping Pre-Test" and have them compare their responses.

Process:

What is the most noticeable change in your responses? (In most cases, the pre-test will be loaded with advice-giving.)

What kinds of questions or situations are still most difficult for you?

In what areas of your training do you feel most confident and in what areas are you most unsure?

Chapter 6

Programs

About three weeks before the peer counselors' training is completed, begin meeting with the counselors and teachers who will be involved in peer counselor programs and placements. This will involve having counselors identify students they would like to refer for group, having elementary counselors and teachers identify students for the "special friend" program, having teachers of emotionally handicapped students identify their students for the high school/junior high special placement program, and so on.

If you will have more than one type of placement occurring on the same day, know how many peer counselors, including how many males and females, will be available for each type of placement before setting up meetings. These numbers will determine how many groups you can offer, how many males and how many females will be available for "special friends," and so on.

In my experience, the most successful placements occur when the peer counselors are given some opportunity to choose the areas in which they will work. Explain all of the placements from which the peer counselors may choose, the responsibilities of each, and how many peer counselors you will need for each placement. After all placement decisions have been made, send the "Placement Notification Letter," located in the Appendix, to the peer counselors' parents with the appropriate placements indicated. These letters *must* be returned before the peer counselors are allowed to begin any placements, especially if the placements require the peer counselors to travel to another school. *Make sure you have administrative support for all peer counselor programs before beginning!*

Develop a procedure for the peer counselors to follow if they are absent on a day of placements. Instruct the peer counselors to call the school where they have their placement, leaving a message for the teacher/counselor and also for the student with whom they work. They are also to call another peer counselor since their absence often affects travel arrangements, and so forth. Make a list of the peer counselors' phone numbers and the phone numbers of all the schools where peer counselors work. An example of this list, "Peer Counselor Phone Tree," is located in the Appendix.

Support Group Program

About three to four weeks prior to the first group, begin advertising the date support groups will begin. In addition to having counselors identify students for the groups, also have the peer counselors begin talking to students they feel would benefit from being in a group.

Run announcements and display posters such as the following:

Student Announcement:
Peer Support Groups are beginning soon! If you'd like to make some new friends and also have a time each week when you can talk about things happening in your life, sign up in the counseling office by November 15.

Poster:
Run copies of the following poster and place one in each faculty mail box, asking a copy be posted in each classroom:

PEER SUPPORT GROUPS
ARE
FRIENDS HELPING FRIENDS

Would you like to have a place to talk about things happening in your life? A place to make some new friends? If so, Peer Support Groups are for you!

SIGN UP IN THE COUNSELING OFFICE
BY NOVEMBER 15!!!

Group Leadership and Support Group Training

1. Have the peer counselors read and discuss "Group Leadership," "Stages in the Life of a Group," "Tips for Group Leaders," and "Giving (and Receiving) Feedback."

2. Explain the dynamics of your group program. In my experience, the most effective support group programs in schools consist of the following elements:

Peer Counselor Facilitated:
Peer counselors, usually in teams of two, are the co-facilitators of the groups. A school or other professional counselor is a member of the group and attends each group session. The professional counselor takes the role of *group member* but is there to provide guidance and expertise when the need arises.

Rotating Schedule During the School Day:
By rotating the schedules for groups throughout the school day, students only miss a particular class once in six weeks. A copy of the group schedule is given to teachers and staff when the groups begin, and another schedule is made at the beginning of a new semester. An example of a rotating schedule of this type, "Peer Counselor Support Group Schedule," is located in the Appendix.

Roll is Taken:
The professional counselor is in charge of seeing roll is taken, and the *presence or absence* of each group member is communicated to teachers. Consistent communication to teachers regarding group attendance is often the weak link in a support group program within a school. Teachers will be much more supportive of a support group program when they know attention is given to seeing students are where they are scheduled to be. Immediately after each group concludes, the professional counselor placès a completed "Peer Counselor Support Group Program Attendance Verification" form for each peer counselor and group member in the appropriate faculty mail box. This form is located in the Appendix.

An "Open" System is Used:

The support group system is "open" rather than "closed." This means new group members may enter a group after it has started, as long as there is room in the group. A group is made available to a student when the need surfaces. An open group system does *not* mean anyone can go to any group anytime! Groups are only open to the group members. Visitors or other "drop-ins" are never accepted.

Open groups continue for the entire school year. This approach avoids the time consuming process of continually starting a new series of groups. My experience is groups of ten or twelve weeks duration are only marginally effective in schools. It usually takes four to six weeks before trust develops among a group of students, since most of them will have had their trust violated by other students at some time. Much of the productive working time for a group of short duration is used up in the developmental stage of the group.

Before new members join a group, the peer counselors in that group meet to extend their welcome and answer questions. New members sign a confidentiality contract during their first group session, and group guidelines are explained. A quick get-acquainted activity will extend the feeling of welcome and belonging. Sometimes new group members seem to blend with a group. Other times new group members stimulate upheaval within the group. Either way, the group members' actions communicate a great deal, and this awareness can be used in the continuing development within the group.

3. Have the peer counselors read and discuss "Ground Rules for Group Sessions" and the "Support Group Confidentiality Contract." Discuss the first group session, "Getting to Know Each Other and What is This Group All About Anyway?", as a way of explaining how the ground rules and the confidentiality contracts are used.

4. Allow the peer counselors to form themselves into teams to co-facilitate groups. Explain to the peer counselors that, as much as possible, the teams are to consist of a male and female, a quiet personality paired with an outgoing personality, an advanced peer counselor paired with a beginning peer counselor, and so on. Allow the team of peer counselors to choose the professional counselor with whom they will work, if possible.

5. Working with the counseling department, begin to arrange the student names into groups. Make every attempt to achieve the best match between students in the group and those who will facilitate the group.

6. Mail a notification letter to the parents or guardians of all students who have chosen to participate in the support group program. A sample letter, "Peer Support Group Parent Notification Letter," is located in the Appendix.

7. As the date for starting support groups approaches, have the peer counselors address notes to their group members, giving them the "who, what, where, and when" information they need:

Your first Peer Support Group will meet _____ period, Tuesday, November 20. We will meet each week in the group room in the counseling office. Please report directly there at the beginning of the period as your teachers have already been notified of your participation. However, you will be responsible for all the material you miss while in group, so it is very important you check with your teacher the day before. SEE YOU AT GROUP!

Individual Referrals

Students may self-refer or be referred by a parent, teacher, counselor, administrator, or friend for individual work with a peer counselor. The "Memo to Faculty/Staff," which explains the referral process by someone other than the student, and the "Peer Counselor Referral" form are located in the Appendix. In all cases, any work with a peer counselor is *always* voluntary for a student.

Although it is preferable for peer counselors to do their individual work with other students during non-school hours, this is often impossible. Most teachers and administrators are relatively comfortable with peer counselors and students working together individually during class time when they are assured it is legitimate and controlled. The form to be used by peer counselors if they need to talk individually with a student during class time is the "Peer Counselor Request For Student" form, which is located in the Appendix.

"Special Friend" Program

Arrange to speak at a faculty meeting at the elementary schools where peer counselors will be working as "special friends." Give copies of the "Peer Counselor Training and Programs" form, located in the Appendix, to the faculty members to explain the scope of the peer counselor program. Discuss peer counselor guidelines for confidentiality and also for required reporting situations, such as abuse or suicidal behavior. Explain the "special friend" program is primarily a prevention program in which elementary students who are seen as being at risk are matched with a peer counselor. The peer counselors meet with their "special friend" at the elementary school once a week for the duration of the school year to provide individual attention and positive role modeling.

Behavior indicative of a need for a "special friend" could be low self-esteem, indicators of alcoholism or other drug abuse in the home, excessive anger or aggressiveness, inability to make friends, difficulty concentrating, and so on.

The students best served are those who are more likely to talk to someone nearer their age. This, of course, is a great many young people. The "special friend" program also works well to serve those students who need more individual attention than can be provided or those who need as extensive a support network as possible, perhaps working with both the elementary counselor and a peer counselor.

Although it is the referring teacher or counselor who completes the "Peer Counselor Special Friend Program Referral," located in the Appendix, requests for "special friends" are also accepted from parents and students. The person making the referral is responsible for obtaining parent permission, since this person usually has the closest working relationship with the student and parents. The "Peer Counselor Special Friend Program Permission Form," located in the Appendix, can be used as a written record of parent permission.

The peer counselors work toward achieving the goals and expectations described on the referral form. In accomplishing this, the peer counselors and their "special friends" must first get to know and trust each other. At first, their time may be spent in get-acquainted activities and playing games together. As the relationship develops, the peer counselors devise activities and discussions which address the issues of the student. Some of these activities may be adaptations of group activities, or they may come from books such as *100 Ways To Enhance Self-Concept in the Classroom*, by Jack Canfield and Harold C. Wells. Peer counselors also frequently devise their own activities for their "special friends."

The peer counselors are required to consult with their "special friend's" teacher twice during a nine- to ten-week grading period. During the consultation, the peer counselors discuss their journal entries for each session. The journal entries include information such as where they usually go to talk with their "special friend," the *general* topics covered, activities used, and plans for future sessions. At this time the teacher is asked to update the peer counselor on any new developments with the student and to provide feedback for the peer counselor on the student's progress.

One of the most heartwarming aspects of this program is seeing there is someone for everyone, and the peer counselors often comment that their "special friend" reminds them of themselves at the same age! After the peer counselors are matched with their elementary "special friends," invite elementary counselors to provide additional in-service training for the peer counselors. This gives the elementary counselors an opportunity to become acquainted with the peer counselors and also to provide additional suggestions for working with their "special friends."

On the first day of the "special friend" program, the elementary counselor meets the peer counselors at the elementary school. The elementary counselor shows the peer counselors such things as where to sign in, and they also give the peer counselors a tour of the building. The elementary counselor takes the peer counselors to the classrooms to meet their "special friend" and the teacher. The peer counselors use this opportunity to make an appointment with the teacher in order to get acquainted before actually beginning the program the following week. By prior arrangement, the "special friends" go with the elementary counselor and peer counselors on the tour. With everyone together, the elementary counselor talks about the school rules so everyone is made aware of them.

Some pointers for peer counselors:
Remember you are functioning as the teacher when you are with your "special friend." See school rules are followed at all times. If you use someone's office, see nothing is disturbed in any way. NO food, drinks, or gum!

You are the one who sets the tone. You are the boss. Know what you want to accomplish each time. Be prepared for the fact your "special friend" may "test" you.

Recognize that your "special friend" may be better with you than with teachers or others. This may make it difficult for you to see the situation from the teacher's or parent's point of view. Work to stay balanced in your perspective.

Remember this is largely prevention work. You may or may not see changes in your "special friend." However, you *will* provide important positive attention, support, and role modeling. Your "special friend" may never tell you in words how one feels about your coming each week. All you have to do is ask yourself how you would have felt at that age if someone had given you this much attention.

Never reveal to your "special friend" anything you have learned from the referral form. Instead, use that information to draw out your "special friend" and to recognize the significance of what is said.

Use self-disclosure often. Share with your "special friend" how you feel about things now and how you felt about things at that age. Share common experiences as well.

If you ever miss a session, a phone call to your "special friend" in the evening will mean a great deal. You may want to exchange phone numbers so your "special friend" can reach you.

Don't promise what you might not do. For example, at the end of the year, don't say "We'll stay in touch" if you are leaving town, unless you are willing to do a lot·of letter writing.

Never, ever leave the school grounds with your "special friend." If you want to take your "special friend" out after school or on the weekend, do so only with the permission of the parents. Always pick your "special friend" up at home and return the child back home. Drive *very carefully* and be especially careful of your choice of activities. Make sure your parents and your "special friend's" parents understand this is extra on your part and is not a part of the school program.

Never share music, books, or anything else that might be seen *by anyone* as a negative or debatable influence upon your "special friend."

Always remember this: The ones that need you the most are often the toughest ones to handle!

Junior High/High School
Special Placement Program

The organization of this program parallels the "special friend" program. Even though this will be the favorite placement for some of the peer counselors, it will be the most challenging placement for many of them. Of course this means when "breakthroughs" do occur, they are just that much more rewarding and heartwarming! However, it often helps the peer counselors to change their focus with this placement. Rather than focusing on changing behavior, it is more helpful with this placement to focus simply on being a friend and "being there." The peer counselors provide a place, often the *only* place, where their students can ventilate feelings, hear other perspectives, and still feel accepted and important. This is an invaluable gift to give to another person!

The in-service provided by the special teacher for emotionally handicapped students will be particularly important. The special teacher can help the peer counselors understand the special needs and problems of these students. The special teacher can share effective ways of responding to the students and also insight into their feelings. This understanding can have an extremely important effect in beginning to create a more accepting environment within a school for a population of students who are often avoided or ostracized.

Classroom Presentations

Fourth Grade Substance Abuse Prevention Program:

The peer counselor substance abuse prevention program is a four session series of presentations by peer counselors on the topics of self-esteem, feelings, communication, and substance abuse. This program is most effective when it functions as part of a comprehensive program of prevention within the school system.

The peer counselors work in teams of two or more, returning each week to the same classroom for the four sessions. The sessions are scheduled during the peer counselor class time, and they occur on a series of four Fridays (or four Mondays). The peer counselors travel to an elementary school to give these presentations.

About a month before the classroom presentations, present the peer counselor substance abuse prevention program at a meeting of elementary principals. Give an overview of the program, along with the dates and times the peer counselors are available. Distribute copies of the "Peer Counselor Fourth Grade Substance Abuse Prevention Program," located in the Appendix. Explain you will send a follow-up memo to get the names of the teachers who will participate but also be prepared to take names at the meeting. The memo, "Substance Abuse Prevention Program Memo to Principals," is located in the Appendix. About two weeks before the presentations begin, send the "Substance Abuse Prevention Program Memo" and "Letter to Teachers" to confirm arrangements.

In preparing for these presentations, the peer counselors take the role of the fourth graders while the peer counselor advisor takes the role of a peer counselor. This way the peer counselors have a model for ways to handle different situations, and they also learn by participating rather than by listening.

Emphasize the peer counselors are to become so familiar with each session they won't need to refer to their presentation material while in the classroom. In the first session, one of the peer counselors will read the story, *Warm Fuzzies*, to the fourth grade students. Encourage the peer counselors to use a lot of *expression* in reading this story. Young people this age love to have people read to them! Also, in the second and third sessions, the peer counselors will be asking for volunteers for demonstrations and role plays. One peer counselor will always work with the volunteers to make sure they understand the instructions while the other peer counselor will keep the rest of the class engaged. The peer counselors need to be very careful to select as many different students as possible as volunteers.

Emphasize the importance of maintaining a positive environment for all the students. One way to provide support and positive feedback for the volunteers is to see they receive applause for their participation. Alert the peer counselors to watch for students who appear to be "put down" by their classmates and have them work to neutralize any such situations as much as possible during the sessions. Explain to the peer counselors if they ever need the classroom teacher's help, they are to ask for it. Generally the teachers will hold back unless they are asked, in order not to interfere.

Each of the sessions uses a "question box" for the students. One peer counselor at the beginning of each session will go through the questions to choose the most important ones. If the questions relate to friends or relationships, the peer counselors may offer suggestions and their own experiences. However, sometimes the peer counselors will receive questions of a serious nature. They are never to try to answer these questions. Instead, they are to *strongly urge* any student with a problem of a serious nature to talk with their teacher or elementary counselor *today!*

Explain to the peer counselors the students will look up to them and will give tremendous weight to everything they say. This implies a tremendous responsibility! Parents report their sons or daughters talk about the peer counselors for weeks after the presentations! The peer counselors have an opportunity to use their influence to help set a standard of acceptance, compassion, and health among a group of young people. This is positive peer pressure in action, and it is one of the most heartwarming and awe-inspiring of all peer counselor activities!

For the last session have certificates to present to the fourth graders to commemorate their completion of this program. The certificates read:

This certifies that

_____

**has successfully completed the
Peer Counselor Substance Abuse Prevention Program.**

The following agreement has been made:

**I agree
I will never abuse alcohol
or any other drug.**

**I also agree
I will do what I can
to get help for any friend who does.**

_____
Student Signature

Witnessed By:

_____   _____
Teacher   **Date**   **Peer Counselor**   **Date**

_____
Peer Counselor Date

Sixth Grade Transition To The Junior High Program

The peer counselor transition to the junior high program is a single session presentation designed to give sixth graders a sense of confidence as they move into the junior high. The presentation includes a discussion of the differences the students will experience at the junior high. This includes instruction in opening a combination lock, since the nightmare of every junior high student is not being able to open the locker! The presentation also includes a rumor control activity and a refusal skills demonstration.

During the "Rumor Control Activity," five volunteers are selected, and four of them leave the room. One peer counselor is to stay with the four volunteers until they have all returned to the classroom.

The peer counselors also design posters with the refusal skills listed on them, and they leave the posters in the classroom after their presentation is finished. This way they are able to extend their "presence" and their influence for a longer period of time. Teachers have reported students refer to these posters until school ends.

The peer counselors work in teams of three or more, so they can divide the class into small groups during the refusal skills activity. The presentation is scheduled during the peer counselor class time together with one other class period. The peer counselors travel to an elementary school to give these presentations. Arrangements for the presentations are made by speaking at a meeting of elementary principals, and organizational materials are located in the Appendix.

Chapter 7

Evaluation

Once the programs and placements have begun, the most important element for maintaining a high level of performance is communication. For this reason, the peer counselors are required to do two consultations each grading period with each professional with whom they are working.

Support Group Program:

The peer counselor group teams are required to consult with the counselor in their group at least twice each grading period. During the consultation, feelings about how the group is progressing are shared, problems within the group are identified, and plans are made for further development within the group.

"Special Friend" Program:

The peer counselors are required to consult with their "special friend's" teacher twice each grading period. During the consultation, the peer counselors share information from their journals, receive feedback or new information from the teacher regarding the student, and further develop goals for the student.

Special Placement Program:

The peer counselors are required to consult with their special placement student's teacher twice each grading period. During the consultation, the peer counselors share information from their journals, receive feedback or new information from the teacher regarding the student, and further develop goals for the student.

Each peer counselor is required to do a total of six consultations each grading period. A due date is set at midterm for the first three consultations with the remaining three consultations being due at the end of the grading period. The peer counselors write a summary of each conference on the "Consultation Report" form, located in the Appendix. In this report, the peer counselors discuss:

1. how they feel about the placement,
2. what kinds of activities they have used and how well they seemed to work,
3. what their goals are for the placement,
4. what feedback they have received from the student and the teacher or counselor, and
5. what they need from the peer counselor advisor.

When the peer counselor advisor returns these reports with a personal message noting strengths the peer counselor is developing, offering support or a different perspective on a situation, or suggesting other possible approaches to a situation, it continues to develop the personal communication between the peer counselor advisor and the peer counselors. This is critically important at this time since much of the work of the peer counselors is now independent of the peer counselor advisor.

At the end of each grading period, a copy of the "Peer Counselor Program Evaluation Form," located in the Appendix, is sent to each teacher and counselor working with a peer counselor. This is important to the professionals as it provides a way for them to communicate with the peer counselor advisor. It also provides a balance in the feedback the peer counselor advisor is receiving on the placements and programs.

The peer counselors' progress in other classes is also monitored by reviewing their grades each grading period. Since the peer counselors miss some time from other classes for their work within the program, this is an important part of the on-going "public relations" work of the peer counselor advisor. This also sends a clear and caring message to the peer counselors of the importance of all areas of their lives, not just those within the scope of the peer counselor program.

Appendix

Challenge Report

Name _____

Challenge:

_____

Challenge:

_____

Challenge:

_____

Challenge:

_____

Challenge:

_____

New Student Buddy Program

Name: Alison Brown

Periods Available: 1-6

Interests/Activities:
I like running, being outdoors, sports, reading all kinds of books, most kinds of music, cooking, camping, and being with my friends. I have my own beliefs, but I'm interested in what others believe, too. I may be a teacher, but I'm not sure yet.

Name: Chad Carson

Periods Available: 1, 2, 4-6

Interests/Activities:
I like snowskiing and waterskiing, hiking, and working on old cars. I am in the choir and in drama club, and I play football and basketball. I have three dogs, two cats, and one parrot. I want to go to State University and study to be a veterinarian.

Name: Cathy Hanson

Periods Available: 1-3, 6

Interests/Activities:
I enjoy walking through the woods or just spending time alone. Talking to people is really easy for me, and I enjoy meeting new people. I was a new student last year, moving here from California. I love to shop and spend money and have fun. My favorite subject is between class socializing.

Name: Johnny Martin

Periods Available: 1-5

Interests/Activities:
I love old movies, politics, and competitive swimming. Sometimes I'm quiet, and sometimes I'm talkative. I am a very talented cook, and I enjoy doing anything with my friends and family. I enjoy football and baseball. The beach is my favorite place to be.

Non-Attending Activity

Speaker:

To give your partner the opportunity to practice the attending skills we just discussed, you will take the role of a friend wanting to talk to a peer counselor. You will start the conversation. You are to talk about a personal habit or characteristic you want to change because it has caused you problems. You will need to talk about five minutes.

Listener:

As your partner begins to talk, demonstrate good attending skills by using the attending behaviors we have discussed.

After your partner has talked for a little while, begin using *poor attending behaviors* such as looking or turning away, tapping your pencil, avoiding eye contact, giving advice, interrupting, topping your partner's story with a better one of your own, etc. Do this as casually as possible so it is not obvious you are doing it on purpose.

Alternate between using good attending skills and poor attending behaviors.

Role Play Topics for Training Triads

You and your parents used to be really close. Lately you hardly spend any time together. It seems like something is always going wrong.

You have been wanting to break up with your boyfriend (girlfriend) for several weeks. However, your boyfriend (girlfriend) says he (she) won't have anything to live for if you leave him (her).

People make fun of you behind your back. When you try to talk to them, they just look at you and walk away. You don't have any friends.

You think you should be allowed to stay out later on weekends and go out on school nights. Your parents say "not until next year."

Your parents got divorced a few months ago. Your dad is always pumping you to find out what your mom is doing. Your mom does the same thing. You keep getting caught in the middle.

Your first hour teacher accused you of cheating and tore up your test. You got an F on the test, but it was the person behind you who was cheating.

Your best friend always asks to sleep over when he (she) wants to go out with a certain person. His (her) parents won't allow him (her) to go out with this person because there has been trouble in the past. Your best friend's parents have always trusted and liked you.

There is this very special guy. You like him more than anyone else you have ever dated. However, he has started pressuring you to have sex. You're just not ready, but you know he'll stop asking you out.

You let a friend borrow your car even though your parents have told you never to do that. He (she) put a dent in the fender. When you talked to your friend about it, he (she) said it was already there.

Your dog (cat) died last night. You have had him (her) since you were six months old.

Your best friends have really gotten into drinking/drugging a lot lately. You know they'll drop you if you don't go along, and you don't have any other friends.

Your parents want you to go into the military after you graduate from high school, but you're not interested. You've been fighting with them about it a lot lately. They say they won't help with college expenses so you better talk to a recruiter.

Your best friend's boyfriend (girlfriend) has been seeing someone else at another school. You just found out about it, but your best friend doesn't know yet.

You've always wanted to be a doctor, but your parents fight so much you can't concentrate on your homework. You're failing most of your classes.

You've been saving for a car for two years. Your dad just lost his job. Now you have to pay all your own expenses.

You have been working since ninth grade to be the starting quarterback when you were a senior. Now it looks like you'll be third string, and the coach is talking about moving you to a new position.

A guy who has a reputation for only wanting one thing from a girl asked you out last Friday night. You knew what people said about him, but you didn't believe it. Nothing happened between you, but you had a really good time. On Monday morning, people are saying he's telling all his friends you had sex with him.

Your parents got divorced when you were little. Your mom dates a lot, and you spend a lot of time with your grandparents. Your mom never seems to have time for you, and there's really no one you can talk to. Lately, you've been cutting classes a lot and partying hard every weekend.

Brian's Story

Everyone breathed a sigh of relief when Brian Smith finally graduated. At 19 years of age, some people were beginning to wonder if he was ever going to make it. Although Brian is very intelligent, he spent most of his energy every day getting out of trouble or getting a date for that night. He always said there was plenty of time to study later. He had more important things to do. His favorite saying was, "Let's go pick up some chicks." This attitude had a tendency to get in the way of his classes.

The administrators at the school knew Brian well. He seemed to be in the office more than he was in class. His mother, Mrs. Johnson, was well-known by the teachers, counselors, and administrators. It seemed someone was always contacting her from the school. Mrs. Johnson appreciated what the school was trying to do, but she never followed through with Brian. Brian always promised her he would be better about staying out of trouble and going to class, and she always thought it would be different this time. He used to brag to his friends he could always count on his mom to get him out of a bind.

Brian is the second of four children. His older sister, Susan, is in college and has always gotten straight As. She was student body president the year she graduated. His younger sister, Jodi, is in the sixth grade, but they never talk because she spends most of her time in her room. The youngest child, Mikey, is in kindergarten, and he idolizes Brian. Mikey's kindergarten teacher has already called Brian's mom several times about how disruptive Mikey is in class. Mr. Johnson is a regional sales representative for a large company, and he is away on business about two weeks out of every month. When he is home, he can usually be found in front of the television with a can of beer. When he and Brian talk, it usually develops into an argument.

In junior high, Brian went out for football. He had a lot of talent and worked hard for a little while. Then he started to cut practice, and the coach told him to turn in his gear. That was the last time Brian got involved with any kind of school activity.

Brian's friends tend to get into trouble a lot. Since Brian has been hanging around with them, he has been getting into fights and running into trouble with the police. Once just before he graduated, the police arrested him and some of his friends at school.

Now that Brian has graduated, he has moved out and is living with friends. He just lost his job, but he says this time he is going to find something where he can work outside and won't have to take orders from anybody. He has had several interviews but no job offers yet.

Placement Notification Letter

Dear Parent or Guardian:

The peer counselors have completed their training. I have arranged placements for them so they will have a variety of opportunities to work with other students. Your son or daughter has chosen to participate in the programs which have been checked. Please notice several of these programs require the peer counselors to leave the high school during the school day.

_____ Counseling support group at _____ one hour per week. The time for the group rotates through the school day: first hour one week, second hour the next week, and so on. The peer counselors work with a school counselor or other professional counselor to facilitate their groups.

_____ Individual work with a "special friend" at _____ elementary school one hour per week during our peer counselor class time.

_____ Individual work with a special education student at _____ one hour per week during our peer counselor class time.

_____ Placement with the alternative high school one hour per week during our peer counselor class time.

_____ Two series of classroom presentations at various elementary schools. The first series in February and March is our Substance Abuse Prevention Program. The second series in April and May is our Transition To The Junior High Program.

In order to travel to the different schools for these placements, your son or daughter will need to ride in a car with me, ride in a car driven by another peer counselor, or drive his or her own car. Please indicate below which travel arrangements meet with your approval. If you would like further information or clarification, please contact me.

Sincerely,

Carol Painter
Peer Counselor Advisor

* *

_____

has my permission to participate in the programs checked
above and to arrange transportation in the following
way(s):
_____ Ride with Carol Painter
_____ Ride with another peer counselor
_____ Drive own car

_____   _____

Parent or Guardian   Date

Peer Counselor Phone Tree

If you are absent on a:

Tuesday:
(1) Call the counselor in your group.
(2) Call your peer counselor team member.

Wednesday:
(1) Call the teacher/counselor with whom you work and leave a message for your student.
(2) Call a peer counselor.

Thursday:
(1) Call the teacher/counselor with whom you work and leave a message for your student.
(2) Call a peer counselor.

Metropolis High School	555-3535
Metropolis Junior High	555-1234
Lincoln Elementary School	555-3323
Adams Elementary School	555-7878
Franklin Elementary School	555-9917
Alternative High School	773-9137
Carol Painter	555-3333
Charles Adams	555-2019
Susan Conrad	555-6676
Cathy Eastan	555-8809
Michael Grayson	555-7690
Mari Hartford	555-0190
Scott Hillman	555-3267
Michelle Keaton	555-4464
Brian Lewis	555-2589
Lori Martin	555-3719
Marti Mitchell	555-7190
Jon Owens	555-7632
Paul Stevens	555-8315
Kelly Williams	555-6859

*All phone numbers and all names of students, counselors, and peer counselors used within this book are fictional.

Peer Counselor Support Group Schedule

Date: January 15
To: Faculty and Staff
From: Carol Painter
RE: Peer Support Group Schedules (revised for second semester)

The students listed below are participating in a support group facilitated by peer counselors under the supervision of a school counselor or other professional counselor. The group members and the peer counselors are responsible for all work missed while in group. Please do not report them absent during these group times as they are asked to report directly to the group. One way to avoid marking students absent for these dates is to place a symbol such as G, for group, in your grade book on each date a student will miss your class for the semester.

In your mail box immediately after group, you will find a note verifying a student was present or indicating a student was absent from group. If a student was absent from group, you will then need to change your attendance roster to reflect that absence.

Please let me know if you have any questions or concerns. Thank you for your support!

Group I
Counselor: Bob Chapman
Peer Counselors: Karen Holden, Jeff Markam

Group Members	Date	Period
David Brown	1/19	3rd
Steve Chavez	1/26	4th
George Cobb	2/2	5th
	2/9	6th
Susan Cornell	2/16	1st
Jenny Gee	2/23	2nd
Kim Littleman	3/1	3rd
Frank Smith	3/8	4th
	3/22	5th
Tracy Turner	3/29	6th
Melissa Williams	4/5	1st
Sheri Young	4/12	2nd
	4/19	3rd
	4/26	4th

Group II
Counselor: Jill Jones
Peer Counselors: Kathy Baker, Lenny Smith

Group Members	Date	Period
Dawn Dawson	1/19	4th
Jim Evans	1/26	5th
Teri Franks	2/2	6th
Kerry Goldman	2/9	1st
Julie Johnson	2/16	2nd
Steve Robinson	2/23	3rd
Sam Sandoval	3/1	4th
Teresa Thompson	3/8	5th
vonna Vaughn	3/22	6th
Tom Wilson	3/29	1st
	4/5	2nd
	4/12	3rd
	4/19	4th
	4/26	5th

Group III
Counselor: Ken Blair
Peer Counselors: Christy Ellsworth, Rod Stevenson

Group Members	Date	Period
Alan Anderson	1/19	5th
Claudia Begay	1/26	6th
Holli Brown	2/2	1st
Julie Forman	2/9	2nd
Michelle Hayes	2/16	3rd
Stephanie Newell	2/23	4th
Jim Patrick	3/1	5th
Maria Rodriguez	3/8	6th
Amanda Rogers	3/22	1st
John Tate	3/29	2nd
	4/5	3rd
	4/12	4th
	4/19	5th
	4/26	6th

Peer Counselor Support Group Program Attendance Verification

TO: _____
　　　　Teacher

_____   _____ was
Student   ID Number

_____ Present during group

_____ Absent during group   on _____during _____.
                              Date   Period

_____
Counselor

Peer Support Group Exit Notification

Date:
To:
From: Carol Painter

_____ is no longer participating in the Peer Support Group Program and should be in class during the scheduled group times. THANKS!

Peer Support Group
Parent Notification Letter

Dear Parent or Guardian:

Your son/daughter has chosen to participate in a counseling support group at Metropolis High School. The group sessions are designed to focus on self-awareness and communication skills, although other topics may be discussed. The groups are conducted by a school counselor, or other professional counselor, along with two or three MHS peer counselors. The peer counselors are students at MHS who were chosen through an intensive selection process and who have received special training. The peer counselors function as positive role models and helpers within the group.

Each group meets once a week for a class period. However, group times are on a rotating schedule. Students miss a different class each week, and they only miss a particular class once in a six week period. The students are responsible for making up all the class work they miss as a result of being in group.

If you have any questions, please contact me at 555-3535.

Sincerely,

Carol Painter
Peer Counselor Advisor

Peer Counselor Support Group Evaluation Form

Please indicate the extent of your agreement or disagreement with each statement below by circling the appropriate letters.

SA: Strongly Agree A: Agree U: Uncertain D: Disagree SD: Strongly Disagree

SA A U D SD 1. The peer counselors were always prepared.

SA A U D SD 2. The peer counselors showed enthusiasm.

SA A U D SD 3. The peer counselors showed my thoughts and feelings were important.

SA A U D SD 4. My ability to understand other people has increased as a result of being in this group.

SA A U D SD 5. My ability to understand myself has increased as a result of being in this group.

SA A U D SD 6. I feel better about myself as a result of being in this group.

SA A U D SD 7. I feel better about the choices I make as a result of being in this group.

The thing I have enjoyed most about the group is....

The thing I have liked least about the group is....

Additional Comments:

Memo To Faculty/Staff

To: Faculty/Staff
From: Carol Painter
RE: Referrals to peer counselors

Forms for referring students for work with a peer counselor can be found in the manila envelope labeled "Peer Counselor Referrals" located next to the faculty mail boxes. Students may choose to talk with a peer counselor individually or to join one of our Peer Support Groups. To make either type of referral, you will need to talk to the students to see if they are interested in working with a peer counselor. It is very awkward for peer counselors to approach students in this way unless the students are expecting a peer counselor to contact them.

Some sample approaches you might use for *individual* referrals are:

"I feel worried about you because it appears you are really depressed some days. I'd like to know you have someone to talk to. We have a program here at school where students who are peer counselors are available to talk with other students. The peer counselors care about people, and they are good at understanding the problems of people their own age. Would you be interested in talking to one of them? Would you like me to arrange for a peer counselor to contact you?"

"I'm concerned about you because it seems like you feel really angry some days. That makes me think there's probably a lot going on for you. I'd really like to know you have someone to talk to. We have a program here...."

A sample approach you might use for a *group* referral is:

"We have a support group program here at our school. Peer Support Groups are really friends helping friends. They provide a place for a group of students to get together once a week to talk about things going on in their lives. Sometimes they do activities in the group to help people get to know each other better, and sometimes people talk about problems they're having here at school or at home. I thought you might really enjoy being in a group. Would you like me to arrange for a peer counselor to contact you?"

When talking to students in a personal way such as this, it is important to describe *what* you see happening rather than *why* you think it is happening. When this is paired with a statement of caring and concern, you will have sent a strong message of acceptance and support that will be very important to students even if they choose not to participate in either type of activity.

When I receive an individual referral from you, I will match the student with a peer counselor. The peer counselor will come to you to arrange a time to meet the student. Then the two of them will work out a time they can get together.

When I receive a group referral from you, a peer counselor will contact the student to explain the group schedule and to answer any questions. Teachers will be notified when a student joins a group.

Please help me by using the Peer Counselor Referral form. It asks for the information I need to make the best possible match, both for individual and group referrals.

Thanks for your involvement!

Peer Counselor Referral

_____ Individual

_____ Group

Name _____

ID No. _____

Please describe the specific behaviors or events you have observed which cause you to be concerned about this student.

How did this student respond to the idea of talking with a peer counselor?

Signature	Date

Please return to Carol Painter

Peer Counselor Request for Student

_____ is requesting time to talk with
Peer Counselor

_____ during ___ period on _____.
Student   Date

_____
Peer Counselor Advisor

Please sign below if this date and time meets with your approval. Both the peer counselor and the student are to report back to their classes by the end of the period.

_____	_____
Teacher Signature (for Peer)	Teacher Signature (for student)
Class Assignment:	Class Assignment:
_____	_____

Peer Counselor Training and Programs

Training

Helper Development
Responsibility
Feelings
Intuition
Advice-Giving
Trying
Being Your Own Best Friend
Projection
Healthy Lifestyle
Fear
Unconditional Love

Skill Development
Attending
Empathy
Clarifying/Questioning
Assertiveness
Confrontation
Problem-Solving

Topic Development
Suicide Prevention and Intervention
Chemical Dependency
Children Of Alcoholics
Grief
Rape
Families
Divorce
Stepfamilies
Teenage Pregnancy
AIDS
Eating Disorders
Family Violence
Stress Management

Programs:
New Student Buddy Program
Individual Referrals
Support Group Program

"Special Friend" Program
Special Placement Program: junior high/high school special education program

Classroom Presentations:
Sixth Grade Transition to the Junior High Program
Fourth Grade Substance Abuse Prevention Program

Peer Counselor
"Special Friend" Program Referral

The peer counselors are available between 10:30 - 11:25 each Thursday to be a "special friend" to your students. To reserve a "special friend" for one of your students, please complete the following information:

Teacher _____ School _____

Student _____ Grade _____ Sex ____

Ethnic Background _____

Please list the special interests of the student.

Describe the personality traits of the student.

Describe the behavior/background of the student, being as specific as possible.

Describe the goals and expectations you have for the peer counselor in working with the student, being as specific as possible.

Date Parent Permission was given _____

Peer Counselor "Special Friend"
Program Permission Form

The Peer Counselor "Special Friend" Program is a program where high school students, who have been specially selected and trained, provide positive support and role modeling to elementary students. The peer counselors and their "special friends" spend a class period together once a week at the elementary school.

Your son/daughter has been selected as someone who would particularly enjoy being a part of the Peer Counselor "Special Friend" Program.

* *

I give permission for ⎯⎯⎯⎯⎯⎯⎯⎯⎯⎯⎯⎯⎯⎯
to participate in this program.

⎯⎯⎯⎯⎯⎯⎯⎯⎯⎯⎯⎯

Parent Signature

⎯⎯⎯⎯⎯⎯⎯⎯⎯⎯⎯⎯

Teacher Signature

The peer counselor's name is ⎯⎯⎯⎯⎯⎯⎯⎯⎯⎯⎯

For further information, please contact:
Carol Painter
Peer Counselor Advisor
555-3535

Please return this form to ⎯⎯⎯⎯⎯⎯⎯⎯⎯⎯⎯

Peer Counselor
Junior High/High School
Special Placement Program Referral

The peer counselors are available between 10:30 - 11:25 each Wednesday to work with students. If you would like to refer one of your students for this program, please complete the following:

Teacher _____ Room_____ School _____

Student _____ Grade _____ Sex ____

Ethnic Background _____

Please list the special interests of the student.

Describe the personality traits of the student.

Describe the behavior/background of the student, being as specific as possible.

Describe the goals and expectations you have for the peer counselor in working with the student, being as specific as possible.

Date Parent Permission was given _____

Peer Counselor Fourth Grade
Substance Abuse Prevention Program

Dates   **Time**
Friday, February 12   10:40 - 11:15
Friday, February 19
Friday, February 26
Friday, March 4

Session I:
The first session will cover the topic of self-esteem and creating a more positive environment for ourselves and others. The peer counselors will tell the story of "Warm Fuzzies and Cold Pricklies" and will guide your students in a discussion of the effects of a person's behavior on others.

Session II:
The second session will expand on the topic of relating better to others by going into greater detail on feelings. Your students will be given a chance to participate as volunteers in demonstrations that show the ways people communicate their feelings.

Session III:
The third session focuses on ways to communicate so people understand how we feel and what we need. This session will also focus on listening as a part of communication.

Session IV:
The fourth session explains when people don't feel good about themselves, when they don't talk about their feelings, and when it is hard for them to communicate what they need from others, they sometimes will turn to drugs as a way of feeling better. The peer counselors will present certificates to your students which include an agreement not to abuse alcohol or other drugs.

The *deadline* for reserving a peer counselor presentation to your fourth graders is *Wednesday, January 13.*

Substance Abuse Prevention Program
Memo to Principals

Date:
To: Elementary Principals
From: Carol Painter
RE: Peer Counselor Presentations to Fourth Grade Classes

Just a reminder the *deadline* for reserving a peer counselor presentation to your fourth grade classes is *Wednesday, January 13.*

Please indicate below your school and the names of the fourth grade teachers who will be participating in this program. Please return this form to me at Metropolis High School.

THANKS!

School: _____

Fourth Grade Teachers' Names:

_____

_____

_____

_____

Substance Abuse Prevention Program
Memo to Teachers

Date:
To:
From: Carol Painter
RE: Peer Counselor Substance Abuse Prevention Program

Just a note to confirm peer counselors will be presenting our Substance Abuse Prevention Program to your students. The program consists of four presentations which will be given on four consecutive Fridays:

February 12
February 19
February 26
March 4

The peer counselors will be in your classroom from approximately 10:40 - 11:15 on each of these dates. Thank you for inviting us!

Substance Abuse Prevention Program
Letter to Teachers

Dear Colleague,

Thank you for your interest in having peer counselors give our Substance Abuse Prevention Program in your classroom. Please have your students make a small sign with their first name on it to put on their desk before the first session. This will allow the peer counselors to call your students by name during the presentations.

Following is an overview of the four sessions to be presented by peer counselors:

Session I:
The first session will cover the topic of self-esteem and creating a more positive environment for ourselves and others. The peer counselors will read the story of "Warm Fuzzies and Cold Pricklies" and will guide your students in a discussion of the effects of a person's behavior on others.

Session II:

The second session will expand on the topic of relating better to others by going into greater detail on feelings. Your students will be given a chance to participate as volunteers in demonstrations that show the ways people communicate their feelings. The discussion will also center on reasons people have for trying to cover up their feelings rather than talking about them.

Session III:

The third session focuses on ways to communicate so people understand how we feel and what we need. This session will also focus on listening as a part of communication. Your students will have an opportunity to volunteer as part of another demonstration activity.

Session IV:

The fourth session explains when people don't feel good about themselves, when they don't talk about their feelings, and when it is hard for them to communicate what they need from others, they sometimes will turn to drugs as a way of feeling better. The peer counselors will present certificates to your students which include an agreement between the peer counselors and the students stating they won't abuse alcohol or other drugs and they will try to get help for any friend who does.

An evaluation form is attached to this letter, and I ask you to mail it to me upon completion of the presentations. Your input is very important to the improvement of this program. Once again, thank you for your interest and support. If you have any questions or concerns, please contact me at 555-3535.

Sincerely,

Carol Painter
Peer Counselor Advisor

Peer Counselor Classroom Presentation Evaluation Form

Dear Colleague,

I am interested in feedback from you regarding the peer counselor presentation in your classroom. This information will be used to determine the level of performance and to indicate any areas of needed improvement. Please complete this form at your earliest convenience and return to me at Metropolis High School.

THANK YOU!

SA: Strongly Agree A: Agree U: Uncertain D: Disagree SD: Strongly Disagree

SA A U D SD 1. The peer counselors were well-prepared for their presentation.

SA A U D SD 2. The peer counselors were able to draw out my students and get them involved.

SA A U D SD 3. My students valued the time spent with the peer counselors.

SA A U D SD 4. I valued the time the peer counselors spent with my students.

SA A U D SD 5. The content of the presentation was appropriate.

Have you seen positive changes in your students as a result of the peer counselor presentation? If yes, please comment specifically on the changes you have observed.

What aspect of the presentation was most effective?

What aspect of the presentation was least effective?

Comments or Observations:

_____   _____

Teacher Signature   Date

Peer Counselor Sixth Grade
Transition to the Junior High Program

Dates (Select One)
Monday, April 25
Monday, May 2
Monday, May 9
Monday, May 16

Time
10:00 - 11:15

Presentation

Part I:
The peer counselors will lead a discussion of the differences your students will experience at the junior high, including dealing with lockers and combination locks. The peer counselors will also discuss the clubs and activities at the junior high and will encourage your students to get involved.

Part II:
The peer counselors will ask for volunteers to do a "Rumor Control Activity" in which they will demonstrate how a story changes as it goes from one person to another. They will encourage your students to recognize the damage done with rumors and to look for positive ways to handle situations of this type.

Part III:
The peer counselors will teach eight "Refusal Skills" to your students and will demonstrate the use of these refusal skills in role play situations. They will divide the class into small groups so each student may practice developing effective refusal skills.

The *deadline* for reserving a peer counselor presentation to your sixth graders is *Thursday, March 31.*

Transition to the Junior High Program
Memo to Teachers

Date:
To:
From: Carol Painter
RE: Peer Counselor Transition to the Junior High Program

Just a note to confirm peer counselors will be presenting our Transition To The Junior High Program to your students on Monday, _____, from 10:00 - 11:15.

We are looking forward to working with your students. Thank you for inviting us!

Transition to the Junior High Program
Letter to Teachers

Dear Colleague,

Thank you for your interest in having peer counselors give our Transition To The Junior High Program in your classroom. Following is an overview of the program presented by peer counselors:

Part I:
The peer counselors will lead a discussion of the differences your students will experience at the junior high, including dealing with lockers and combination locks. The peer counselors will also discuss the clubs and activities at the junior high and will encourage your students to get involved.

Part II:
The peer counselors will ask for volunteers to do a "Rumor Control Activity" in which they will demonstrate how a story changes as it goes from one person to another. They will encourage your students to recognize the damage done with rumors and to look for positive ways to handle situations of this type.

Part III:
The peer counselors will teach eight "Refusal Skills" to your students and will demonstrate the use of these refusal skills in role play situations. They will divide the class into small groups so each student may practice developing effective refusal skills.

An evaluation form is attached to this letter, and I ask you to mail it to me upon completion of this presentation. Your input is very important to the improvement of this program. Once again, thank you for your interest and support. If you have any questions or concerns, please contact me at 555-3535.

Sincerely,

Carol Painter
Peer Counselor Advisor

Peer Counselor Program
Evaluation Form

Dear Colleague:

I am interested in feedback from you regarding the Peer Counselor Program and the impact a peer counselor has had on one of your students. This information will be used to determine the level of performance within the program and to indicate any areas of needed improvement.

Please complete this form at your earliest convenience and return to me at Metropolis High School. Thank you for your support and your interest in working with a peer counselor!!

Peer Counselor's Name _____

SA:Strongly Agree A:Agree U:Uncertain D:Disagree
SD:Strongly Disagree

SA A U D SD   1. The peer counselor was dependable and consistent in attendance.

SA A U D SD   2. My student valued the time spent with the peer counselor.

SA A U D SD   3. I valued the time my student spent with the peer counselor.

SA A U D SD   4. I have seen positive changes in my student as a result of working with the peer counselor.

SA A U D SD   5. The student's parents have seen positive changes as a result of having their child work with the peer counselor.

The peer counselors are to make an appointment to meet with you at least twice each grading period to discuss the progress of your student. How satisfactorily has this been done? Comments or suggestions?

_____

Teacher Signature

THANK YOU!

Consultation Report

Peer Counselor Name

Date of Conference

Teacher/Counselor Name

Specify Placement (Support
Group, "Special Friend,"
Special Placement, etc.)

Circle One: In Person,   By Phone

Summary of Conference:

Peer Counselor
Individual Referral Data

Name of Student: _____

Date of Conference: _____ **Grade:** _____

Ethnic Background: _____

Topic Discussed (Please check one or more):

☐ Substance   ☐ Parent/Family ☐ School
  use/abuse
                 ☐ Friends/Social ☐ Sexual/Pregnancy

☐ Other _____
                              (Please Specify)

Referred By (Please check):

☐ Administrator ☐ Counselor   ☐ Teacher

☐ Friend   ☐ Self-Referral

Session (Please check):
☐ 1st   ☐ 2nd   ☐ 3rd   ☐ 4th   ☐ 5th   ☐ 6th

☐ 7th   ☐ 8th   ☐ 9th   ☐ 10th   ☐ Other _____
                                        (Please specify)

_____   _____
Peer Counselor   Date

Peer Counselor
Letter of Recommendation

To Whom It May Concern:

I am pleased to introduce you to a very special young man—Jeffrey Scott. Jeff is a person for whom I have great respect and affection, and this comes as a result of working closely together this year. Jeff is an outstanding member of the Metropolis High School Peer Counselor Program.

Students are chosen as peer counselors only after an extensive screening process, involving both teacher and student evaluation, and an interview before a panel of school counselors and peer counselors. Once selected, the peer counselors receive over fifty hours of special training in helping philosophy, relationship and communication skills, and topics such as suicide prevention and intervention, chemical dependency, grief, and many others.

Jeff worked individually with high school, junior high, and elementary students. He also facilitated a counseling support group at the high school level. In addition, he gave classroom presentations to fourth graders as part of our Substance Abuse Prevention Program and to sixth graders as part of our Transition To The Junior High Program.

Jeff is a person of deep compassion who demonstrates a willingness to reach out to others. He has clear academic and personal goals which he achieves through a strong sense of responsibility and commitment. He is warm, genuine, and unique in his depth of understanding. I feel he is strongly deserving of acknowledgment, and I recommend him to you with pride.

Sincerely,

Carol Painter
Peer Counselor Advisor

National Peer Helpers Association
Membership Application

An annual membership in the National Peer Helpers Association includes a subscription to the *Peer Facilitator Quarterly*. Complete the form below and send with your check for $35 to become a member of this organization. The only way to be placed on the mailing list and to receive updates on conferences and other professional developments is to become a charter member. Don't delay! Join today!

Name: _____

Position: _____

Institution: _____

Address: _____

City : _____ **State:** _____ **Zip Code:** _____

Please make your $35 check payable to NPHA and send it to:

National Peer Helpers Association
P.O. Box 335
Mountain View, CA 94042

References

Canfield, J. and Wells, H.C. (1976). *100 ways to enhance self-concept in the classroom.* Englewood Cliffs, NJ: Prentice-Hall, Inc.

Canning, J. (1985). *Play times: A structured developmental play program utilizing trained peer facilitators.* Minneapolis, MN: Educational Media Corporation.

Drye, R., Goulding, R. and Goulding, M. *No suicide decisions: Patient monitoring of suicidal risk.* American Journal of Psychiatry, 1973, 130, 171-174.

Egan, G. (1975). *The skilled helper.* Monterey, CA: Brooks/Cole Publishing Company.

Foster, E.S. (1983). *Tutoring: Learning by helping.* Minneapolis, MN: Educational Media Corporation.

Ivey, A.E. and Authier, J. (1978). *Microcounseling.* Springfield, IL: Charles C. Thomas.

Joan, P. (1986). *Preventing teenage suicide: The living alternative handbook.* New York, NY: Human Sciences Press, Inc.

Miller, M. (1989). *Suicide. The preventable death.* San Diego, CA: The Information Center.

Myrick, R.D. and Bowman, R.P. (1981). *Becoming a friendly helper: A handbook for student facilitators.* Minneapolis, MN: Educational Media Corporation.

Myrick, R.D. and Bowman, R.P. (1981). *Children helping children: Teaching students to become friendly helpers.* Minneapolis, MN: Educational Media Corporation.

Myrick, R.D. and Erney, T. (1978). *Caring and sharing: Becoming a peer facilitator.* Minneapolis, MN: Educational Media Corporation.

Myrick, R.D. and Erney, T. (1979). *Youth helping youth: A handbook for training peer facilitators.* Minneapolis, MN: Educational Media Corporation.

Myrick, R.D. and Sorenson, D.L. (1988). *Peer helping: A practical guide.* Minneapolis, MN: Educational Media Corporation.

Satir, V. (1983) *Conjoint family therapy.* Palo Alto, CA: Science and Behavior Books.

Tindall, J.A. and Gray, H.D. (1985). *Peer counseling: An in-depth look at training peer helpers.* Muncie, IN: Accelerated Development, Inc.

Tindall, J.A. and Gray, H.D. (1985). *Peer power: Becoming an effective peer helper.* Muncie, IN: Accelerated Development, Inc.

Varenhorst, B. (1980). *Curriculum guide for student peer counseling training.* Palo Alto, CA.

Varenhorst, B. (1983). *Real friends: Becoming the friend you'd like to have.* San Francisco, CA: Harper & Row, Publishers.

Wegscheider, S. (1981). *Another chance: Hope and health for the alcoholic family.* Palo Alto, CA: Science and Behavior Books.